TO ACT JUSTLY

Reflections of Ireland at the end of the Millennium

TO ACT JUSTLY

Reflections of Ireland at the end of the Millennium

Edited by Michael Casey

the columba press

First published in 1999 by

the columba press

55a Spruce Avenue, Stillorgan Industrial Park, Blackrock, Co Dublin
in association with
The Society of St Vincent de Paul

Designed at Language
Printed in Ireland by ColourBooks Ltd, Dublin

ISBN 1-85607-260-6

Acknowledgements
The publisher gratefully acknowledges the permission of the following to use material in their copyright:
Faber and Faber Ltd for the quotations from Seamus Heaney on pp 29 and 66; Beacon Press, Boston for the quotation from Mary Oliver on p 109; Peter Hames and Folkus Music for the quotation from *Ordinary Man* on page 88; HarperCollins, NY and San Francisco for the quotations from *Earthprayers from Around the World* on pages 100/101. Every effort has been made to trace copyright holders. If however we have inadvertently used material without permission, the copyright holder is invited to contact us so that it can be put right in future editions.

CONTENTS

SECTION TWO : GROUPS

SECTION THREE : UNEQUAL SOCIETY

Welcome

It gives me great pleasure to welcome readers to this book of fifty-two reflections, edited by Michael Casey. The reflections cover the themes of poverty, discrimination, exclusion, inequality and injustice. The Society of St Vincent de Paul offers it as one of our contributions to the millennium, the 2000th anniversary of the birth of Christ.

The primary purpose of the book is to raise awareness about these issues among the members of the Society of St Vincent de Paul. It is hoped that the book will also contribute to debate, dialogue and action in the wider Irish society. I believe that the contents could be of particular value and relevance to Community Development Groups, Schools, Social Action or Justice Groups, Parish Newsletters or Church Groups.

In conclusion, may I thank the contributors from all walks of Irish society, who gave so generously of their time, talents and creativity.

I would also like to thank Michael Casey for his key role in making this book a reality.

Noel Clear
National President
Society of St Vincent de Paul

February 1999

THANKS

The contributors have made this book. Thanks to each one of them for their generous response.

Thanks to Phyllis Park for her central contribution in the preparation of the text and her constant support.

Thanks to Mary Whelan for her inspiration and her ideas around creating a book of reflections.

Within the Society of St Vincent de Paul, a special thanks to Larry Tuomey, who facilitated the project and to Monica O'Reilly and Maura Mulhall, who read and commented on the first draft. Warm thanks to all the staff at SVP Headquarters who were so welcoming and good humoured.

Adam May and David Joyce have encapsulated the core and spirit of the reflections in their creative design. Sean O Boyle of Columba Press has been professional and flexible as always. Thanks to all of them.

Michael Casey

Introduction

To act justly, to love tenderly and to walk humbly with your God (Micah Ch 6,v8).

The reflections in this book offer us a cameo view of Irish society at the end of the second millennium. As we look at ourselves through the lens of poverty, discrimination, exclusion, inequality and injustice, what we see is a serious challenge to us as a modern enlightened democracy.

The fifty-two reflections, from such a varied selection of people from around Ireland, provide a very vivid and stark picture. The tapestry woven together from different threads of Irish life, many hidden and unseen in the past, is a sombre winter-coloured one. As with many winter landscapes, it is illuminated with shafts of light, the light of courage, of hope and of justice.

Themes

The tapestry shows three strong themes underlying the wealth of information and experience contained in the fifty-two reflections. The three themes are:

(1)   Irish Society is a structurally divided, unequal society.
(2)   There are specific groups of people who experience exclusion and inequality.
(3)   Individuals have personal experience which reflects the injustice and discrimination of the wider society.

This book is organised into three sections around these three themes: the first section is about personal experience; the second expresses the experience of excluded groups; the third is about the kind of society we are.

Call to Action

The book is also a collective call to action. Many of the contributors feel that the time is *now*. The financial indicators are right; the human and ethical imperatives are there; the analysis is done and there is sufficient national consensus to support the building of a more inclusive, just and equal society. So why isn't this happening?

On Reflection

People from all over Ireland wrote these reflections. Though pressed for time, many of the contributors commented on how valuable the exercise was for them. Being asked to write a *reflection* caused them to reflect about themselves, their lives and their work. This was quite different from being asked to write an article or an essay on the topic.

This is not just a book of readings with facts and figures to be read once and then seen as read. Reading is not the same as reflection. When something is read, especially if it is read quickly, it goes through the logical, rational brain and is judged to be good, interesting, awful! Reading is more for information. But if something is read slowly and meditatively, with a pause at a word or phrase that catches the attention, and if it is allowed to touch the feelings and speak to the spirit, it is being read reflectively. It is hoped that this book will be read reflectively and will move people's souls and spirits as well as their minds.

It is not easy to be reflective or to live a reflective life today. The frantic pace of modern living, stress, competitiveness, media bombardment, are all contributory factors. To be reflective we need to slow down, to create space, to change our whirring minds down a few gears, to take time. Reflection can be encouraged through contact with nature, going for a walk, music, finding a sacred space in your house, church, or doing whatever you find best for you.

Reflective reading

From time immemorial, monks and contemplatives of different religions have done what they called *Lectio Divina,* literally 'divine reading' or 'reading about the divine'. This generally would be from the Scriptures or Holy Books. *Lectio Divina* is a type of reflective reading which leads to contemplation and union with the divine and the whole of the universe. It is meant to be a centering and rooting of one's life in the deeper realities of spirit, soul, the earth, the unity of all humanity, and lead to an inclusive world view.

Reflective living

Lectio Divina is more than reading holy or spiritual books. It is certainly that, but it is also the reading of the book of the universe and the book of everyday life with all its problems and achievements. The divine script is written in the story of the universe and in the stories of people's lives, with their joys and sorrows, their aspirations, disappointments and disasters. This book of reflections is an attempt to awaken us to the presence of the divine in the struggle of peoples' lives, in the competitiveness of the market place, in politics and in the happenings of every day, especially the happenings of the hidden Ireland. Many of the stories are about the dark side of Irish life. This shadow side of our society is reflected in accounts of violence against women, rejection and mistreatment of refugees, racism, homelessness and many others. The contributors represent individuals or groups who have experienced the dark. Their stories are a challenge to each one of us individually, and to us as a society, to engage with the darkness in our midst as we approach the third millennium.

Surely as we approach the year 2000, our Millennium Manifesto as a nation must be to become a more welcoming, just, caring, inclusive Irish society.

Michael Casey

We should seek to recognise the potential of people who have not yet made their voice heard, listen to them and enable them to achieve their goals.

PERSONAL EXPERIENCE

WHO CARES?

Stretching herself too thin, she breaks her connections. Staying too busy, she has no time.
Doing for others, she neglects herself. Defining herself only through others, she loses her own definition.
The wise woman waters her own garden first.

There are some people who can never have the luxury of watering their own garden first. These are "The Carers" in our society. Their garden is taken over by the people for whom they care. It may be a dependent old person or child who is never going to be able to cope with life on their own. These people get drained of life in the caring for others. Often they carry their cross alone and it is a lonely journey.

Sometimes in life when a parent becomes dependent, it is left to one member of the family to cope. The rest abandon ship. They are too busy! If we are the neighbour of such a person how much moral support do we give? Do we not want to get involved in case it would make too many demands on our time? Could we help a little in the carrying of the burden? As a society are we providing enough financial support for Carers? If their charges were being cared for by the state it would cost far more. Our church services could include special prayers for Carers. People need to be supported and confirmed in what they are doing.

I sought my soul,
But my soul I could not see,
I sought my God,
But my God eluded me.
I sought my brother
And I found all three.

Alice Taylor,
Author

Violence and Peace in Ireland

There is a question to be answered one day as to how far the BBC - and Fleet Street too - was responsible for not informing the rest of the country of the conduct of public affairs in Northern Ireland in the fifties and sixties.

British Broadcaster, Alasdair Milne

I was born at 41 Leenan Gardens, Creggan Estate, Derry, on March 3, 1956. I had a relatively happy childhood amongst, without exaggeration, some of the best neighbours in the world. The Creggan Estate was a socially deprived area with high unemployment. Despite this, the Royal Ulster Constabulary will confirm it had one of the lowest crime rates in Western Europe. As children, we had no idea our homes and streets had been deliberately built on the side of a hill in order to corral Catholic votes in Derry within a restricted electoral ward. Gerrymandering, the deliberate rigging and manipulation of the 'democratic' franchise, ensured that the one-third Unionist population of our predominately Nationalist city, ruled with an iron and arrogant will until the late 1960s.

I recall very clearly the first political question I ever asked. I was just twelve years old when I looked with incomprehension at pictures on our black and white television set of RUC officers, some of them quite elderly, viciously beating peaceful Civil Rights demonstrators with batons. "Why?" I asked. It was the 5th of October 1968. Little did those officers realise, acting as they were for their political masters, the first skull they cracked open awakened a sleeping giant.

The so-called 'Troubles' erupted that day and set in motion a chain of events which was to rock the island of Ireland to its foundations. Landmarks were to emerge which would leave indelible scars on the psyche of new generations: Bloody Sunday, Bloody Friday, The Dublin/Monaghan Bombings, Enniskillen, Greysteel, to name but a few. Each atrocity inflicting incalculable suffering and heartache. Each providing rhymes and reasons for those who supported the use of violence and those who opposed it.

In the summer of 1972, in the aftermath of Bloody Sunday, I confronted the killer instinct which lurks within us all. A Grenadier Guard so humiliated me in front of my friends that I know, to this very day, I would have willingly blown his brains out, if I had a gun. The cold chill which possessed me that afternoon so disturbed me I retreated to my home and remained there for three whole days until I was sure I had exorcised the demon from my being.

Then, one Sunday morning in 1979, I witnessed the consequences of a violent act which, in a strange sense, became my salvation and convinced me that violence was not the way forward in the just and noble cause of a united Ireland. I was a volunteer at an alcohol and drug abuse rehabilitation centre on Northland's Road, Derry. At about 10 a.m., I was awakened by four shots and a scream. I dressed quickly and ran outside. About fifty metres away I found a man who had just been assassinated. He lay close to the kerb, his warm blood pouring like paint on to the pavement. Standing over him were his teenage son and daughter. They clasped one another in shocked horror as they stared at the slain body of their father with whom, only minutes before, they had been walking to church. In that moment I realised that violence does not inflict physical wounds alone but also spiritual and historical wounds that can go on from generation to generation. Over 3,000 deaths and 30,000 injuries in 30 years has inflicted unfathomable wounds and hurt. Yet, we stand now on the threshold of a new beginning where, hopefully, dialogue and not destruction has gained the ascendancy. As wounded healers we must walk the road of truth, forgiveness, healing and fear together. All of us, but especially politicians, lawmakers and social commentators, must never forget the fact that Justice and Human Rights are the foundations upon which a peaceful and stable society are built.

Let every word be the fruit of action and reflection. Reflection alone without action is mere theory, adding its weight when we are overloaded with it already and it has led the young to despair. Action alone without reflection is being busy pointlessly. Honour the Word eternal and speak to make a new world possible.
                                                                                              Dom Helder Camara

                                                                                              Don Mullan,
                                                                                              Author

A Place to call Home

The desire for a place to call home is the deepest need in every human heart and perhaps the least recognised.

Sr Stanislaus Kennedy, President, Focus Ireland, 1997

When you are in a hostel, you can't go to the bedroom during the day. You can't put your child to bed for a nap when she needs it. You can't even make a cup of tea when you feel like it.

You have to share a room, it could be with anybody, an alcoholic or somebody with a psychiatric problem. No disrespect to anyone, but there are things you would like to be able to protect your children from, that you feel they are too young to have to deal with, but you have no choice, no control over who you mix with, you are just lumped in with everyone. Somebody we were sharing with overdosed, and my kids had to watch her being carried out like that.

My little girl said we were like goldfish in a shark pool. She was only a child, but she could see that was the situation we were in.

Kate

When you are homeless your self-esteem and your feeling of self-worth takes an awful battering, because you are always justifying yourself, and all the time, you are having to get on with living as well, dealing with three children, living in a hostel, which is not ideal.

Between the time I first went to the hostel and the time I was eventually housed, I felt as if I had been physically walked on, as if my body had been through a wringer. If I hadn't been a strong person, I feel I could have ended up with my kids being taken into care.

One thing that stands out for me is the feeling of helplessness. It's like being in a tunnel. You can't go left or right, all you can do is go forward and do what the authorities say. I know that if I had an address, I would not be treated in the same way. It's as if you are wearing a label, a big banner, saying HOMELESS. The sense of well being you have about keeping a home is gone. I was aware of the stigma attached to being homeless.

Mary

What do you think you would do if you were put into Kate's or Mary's situation?
What do you think you should be doing to give a home to people who need emergency accommodation?
What can you do to ensure that everyone has a right to a home?

Kate and Mary

The Channel of Blessings

Blessed are the merciful: for they shall obtain mercy.
Blessed are the pure in heart: for they shall see God.
Blessed are the peacemakers: for they shall be called the children of God.
Blessed are they who are persecuted for righteousness' sake:
for theirs is the Kingdom of Heaven.

Matthew, Ch 5, v 7-10.

We need to break the silence over racism against refugees in Irish Society. We must stand against any type of discrimination which tends to take over this Irish society. We need to repent of our silence and do something! Let us be the channel of blessings for the nations, regardless of people's origins, colour of skin or status.

I look at myself as that unfortunate person who came from a dark world to an unknown destination. Since I arrived in this country, I first felt lost, without hope, without a sense of a meaningful future. Many questions rose in my head: to know how I will be able to integrate into this community - where a different culture, language were such barriers. But thanks to God! In spite of all the stress on my arrival, God always helps us - bringing the meaning and support we require. I felt again a sense of hope around me and my family.

From that experience I have noticed that our society has to be one which is able to offer a real support to those who are rejected, humiliated, even tortured, because of their beliefs.

A society which is full of merciful people can bring hope to those who are hopeless. This is what we learn from the life of Jesus, who came to bring light to those who are in darkness.

Lord Jesus, help me to identify myself with you at this special time in human history,
so that I will be a blessing for this country where I have come to live.

Nicole Ekoda,
from Congo-Kinshasa,
now living in Dublin

They even stole my Rosary Beads

Nowadays, I'm afraid inside the flat as well as outside.

I never go out once the darkness comes. I get my messages early in the day and stay in. I miss going around to the church. I used to love to sit in front of the Sacred Heart - tell him my troubles, light a lamp - it put in the day and I felt better afterwards. Now the church is closed, and if I go to Gardiner Street, I'm always afraid someone is going to come out from behind the pillars or the confession boxes and grab my purse.

I was poor long ago, but happy now the pension is good but I'm poorer, because I am always nervous. I was broken into twice.

They knock on the door and pretend they are from the Corporation or the Gas Company. I never open it. One fellow kept calling but I gave a description of him to the Guards, and they picked him up in the flats.

I'm much happier since I came into the hospital. I miss my own hall door and making a cup of tea when I like, but I feel safer and that is all that matters.

I worked all my days - paid my way - looked after my mother she was ninety-three years old when she died. One day I was mugged, knocked to the ground, my pension taken and my glasses broken. They even stole my rosary beads - I hope they are using them - I never go out now and I miss it. I used to love, on a Saturday, going around to put a few bob on a horse. I miss all that and it is lonely - they not only robbed me of my money, they took my joy away.

Why isn't there more respect for the elderly today?

Josie

THE SVP IN THE THIRD MILLENNIUM

You give but little when you give of your possessions. It is when you give of yourself that you truly give.

Kahlil Gibran

The Society of St Vincent de Paul will enter the third millennium as an organisation which, for nearly two hundred years has operated as the voice of the poor. How strong, weak or even non-existent that voice is at any time depends on the contribution of each individual member. The material help we give is very important and very often makes a substantial difference to people; material help alone, if that is all we give, tends in time to make our giving harsh and judgmental.

As the second millennium draws to a close it offers a wonderful opportunity to each of us to reflect on our contribution or lack of it to being the voice of the poor and to pledge ourselves to making the SVP a strong voice in the third millennium.

Being a real voice of the poor is no easy task. It involves more than material aid, it involves giving of myself not just while doing my Vincentian work, but allowing being a member of the SVP to affect all my attitudes, words and actions every day.

How important it is then when I am in contact with those whose voice I am, that I listen beyond the words and appearances so that I may be able to "walk in the moccasins of the other". It is a unique privilege that someone allows me to be their voice. If I am honest with myself, I will admit how often I fail in that charge.

On my own, even with the help of my Vincentian colleagues, my task would be an impossible one without strength beyond myself. This is why prayer and reflection on my work is so vital - it enables me to look for the Spirit of God alive, both in those I visit and my fellow Vincentians. It allows me to stay faithful even without any apparent success in the work at times.

How can we move on from being a voice for the poor to help them to speak and act for themselves?

Maura Mulhall,
Member of the Society of St Vincent de Paul

Losing a Loved One

As the century turns, my predominant memory and at times preoccupation, is of the death of my brother Aidan on Thursday, August 29, 1991. He was killed at noon when the front of his company van collapsed and he careered under the front of an oncoming truck. Another woman also died in the carnage.

I remember Aidan being born just after the Angelus bell tolled on RTE. As "Labhair Gaeilge Linn" began on our TV, we could hear his first cries upstairs. Almost to the day, he was ten years younger than me. In a large family I was at a good age to push his pram and "mind" him. His death for me is a wound that will never heal.

He was a good smart lad, but we had to physically drag him to school, kicking and screaming. Myself and our next door neighbour dreaded this early morning ritual - at that stage his physical protestations had become too much for my mother. I only realised later that it wasn't school he hated - far from it, but the fear of leaving my mother at home on her own.

And so since he was killed, aged twenty-five years, I now realise that one of the ways I have grieved is through events of the century that have taken so many young men of a similar age. I have since visited many, many graves in France and Belgium from the First World War. There are so many "Duffys" even some "A. Duffys", you will find your own name there. And, likewise, the Vietnam Memorial in Washington. War veterans sell dog tags - of course there was one with Aidan's date of birth, 19.1.66., and often our own national war memorial in Islandbridge in Dublin which also has list after list of names. There is something living and longing in these lists.

Even after the horrific Omagh bombing on August 15, 1998, which I covered in the course of my work, a local priest in the town wrote to me to acknowledge the media - and had the grace and generosity to remember Aidan as well.

It is the same propulsion that draws me to Seamus Heaney's poem, *Mid-Term Break*.
It talks of an older brother's loss and the deep hurt the death of a young person can visit on a family.

MID-TERM BREAK

(Seamus Heaney)

I sat all morning in the college sick bay
Counting bells knelling classes to a close.
At two o'clock our neighbours drove me home.

In the porch I met my father crying -
He had always taken funerals in his stride -
And Big Jim Evans saying it was a hard blow.

The baby cooed and laughed and rocked the pram
When I came in, and I was embarrassed
By old men standing up to shake my hand
And tell me they were 'sorry for my trouble';
Whispers informed strangers I was the eldest,
Away at school, as my mother held my hand

In hers and coughed out angry tearless sighs.
At ten o'clock the ambulance arrived
With the corpse, stanched and bandaged by the nurses.

Next morning I went up into the room.
Snowdrops and candles soothed the bedside; I saw him
For the first time in six weeks. Paler now,

Wearing a poppy bruise on his left temple,
He lay in the four foot box as in his cot.
No gaudy scars, the bumper knocked him clear.

A four foot box, a foot for every year.

Joe Duffy,
Broadcaster
Radio Telefis Eireann

Empowerment

I am first and foremost unlearned, an unlettered exile who cannot plan for the future.
I was like a stone lying in the deep mud. Then he who is mighty came and in his mercy he not only pulled me out
but lifted me up and placed me at the top of the wall.

St Patrick's Confession - trans. Joseph Duffy

For a number of years I have worked along with different community groups in disadvantaged and troubled areas of Northern Ireland, which have come together to try and improve the quality of life of their local community. The groups have an approach which helps people to identify their own needs and empowers them to work towards meeting them in their own way. Empowerment means actively offering support and friendship to people who have been excluded and building their confidence and self esteem, so that they can take up opportunities to learn new information and skills. People see that they can do things they never thought possible, such as: writing their own poems and stories, using a computer, speaking on a local radio programme, taking an active part in their local community and arguing their case to statutory agencies. Group members take pride in each other's achievements. The groups themselves are also empowered by their collective experiences and move on to further stages of development.

Empowerment gives people a voice to speak for themselves and have a sense of their own identity and power. It begins with a small step, but people working together can then move on to make real changes for their community. The early Celtic church to which Patrick spoke, was one based on the values of community. He moved from the excluded powerless position of a slave to a place at "the top of the wall" and became a voice and support for his community.

We should seek to recognise the potential of people who have not yet made their voice heard, listen to them and enable them to achieve their goals.

Liz McShane,
Community Development & Research Consultant Belfast

My Recovery from Drugs

The SAOL Project is a two year pilot programme for former and stable women drug users whose purpose is to move, through development work and capacity building, from addiction and dependency to self direction and self reliance. It operates on the basis of social justice, adult education and community development principles, and focuses on re-integration into the community. SAOL stands for Seasamhacht, Abaltacht, Obair, Léann. The SAOL project is based in Amiens Street in Dublin.

....Just two years ago I was a nobody, or so I thought. The SAOL tutors did a lot of work with me and the other girls on social skills, equality, opportunities and the chance to make changes in our lives. The first thing we did was to look at our self worth. I had none myself. When you have been treated by the system the way I have, you would know what I mean. I have been a drug addict most of my life. I did not get off to a great start when I was young. I went to school in Rutland Street; the classes were very packed and there were about forty kids to a class. I got to learn very little and I left there when I was only eleven years old.

I began to take heroin around the same time and that was it for me for the next fifteen years. I spent those years bound over to a Drug Treatment Centre in Jervis Street Hospital. The best thing that ever happened to me was when I was given a place on the City Clinic Methadone Maintenance Programme. The staff there were very caring and supportive in many ways. I attended there for two years without ever stepping out of line in any way. The staff there put my name down for the SAOL course when it became available. The staff in SAOL are the most down to earth people I have ever met. They came from working class backgrounds and knew all about life and other struggles. It was a bit strange in the beginning when I realised that the staff were showing me trust. I never felt this from anyone. No one ever trusts addicts. Society never lets you forget and society never forgives - or so I thought. But SAOL gave me the key to my freedom. I felt like I had been released from a prison. I mean, people don't formally put you in prison, but they strip you of rights and self esteem and you end up in prison within yourself.

The people in SAOL treated us as equals and that meant that we had a lot of rights as well as a lot of responsibilities. We had a say in every part of the programme; we could call a meeting anytime if we wanted to challenge someone or something. We were always encouraged to speak on our own behalf. We always went to seminars and even to the National Drug Task Force to make our own case.

I was the SAOL representative on the Inter Agency Drugs Project. My boss, Joan, just told me to be myself, that it was time people heard from our side of the fence. So there I was, sitting at the same table as doctors, politicians, gardaí and counsellors. Believe it or not, they treated me just like one of themselves. I began to speak up for other drug users. I began to speak about what needed to change so that we could get our fair share. I spoke about housing, discrimination and the way we are treated by the doctors and hospitals. I said that education was important for drug users, we never had any; we also needed decent treatment from the social services. We didn't want to see history repeating itself for our own kids. Most of the things I said to this group have been taken on as recommendations by the Local Drugs Task Force.

Anna Keogh,
Peer worker, SAOL project

Standing in God's Presence

To stand in your presence and serve you.

The woman spoke of her utter delight when she was offered a flat (her first home) by the Corporation. As she entered the flats complex for the first time with her husband and two small children, her hope for the future turned quickly to despair. In that moment she became suddenly and acutely aware of what lay ahead. Her spirit of hope had little chance of surviving in the concrete bleakness of the flats. She explained that "you can't have faith in the flats" - faith in yourself, faith in other people or faith in God. As she struggled to raise her family over the years she was supported by members of the local Saint Vincent de Paul Conference. Twenty years later she told me that she was finding her way back to herself, to accepting other people as they are and, recognising now some good things in her life, was turning more to God. She has now found some measure of peace. The friendship of people who cared had made the difference.

It is a natural reaction to despair in the face of misery and injustice. The spirit of hope is the antidote I need. Standing in God's presence changes moments of despair into moments where I can catch glimpses of hope. My Vincentian work of service is often difficult and requires patience and dedication to the 'long haul'. Can it ever be about the 'quick fix'? Often I encounter situations in my work which raise questions I cannot answer. Standing in God's presence helps me to face these questions. It colours my life, my work and all its challenges.

I can so easily fall into the trap of believing that I am serving God and my neighbour when, in fact, I am serving no more than my own needs and self interest. Standing in God's presence I become aware of the difference.

Lord, what is the point of your presence if our lives do not alter?
Change our lives. Shatter our complacency.
Take away that self regard which makes our consciences feel clear.
Press us uncomfortably.
For only thus that other peace is made.
Your peace.

Helder Camara.

Monica O'Reilly,
Member of Ethos Development Group, SVP.

Only the Telly to talk to

You can live in the middle of people and feel completely alone.

I am living on my own in the city and I am very lonely ... every day. All my mother's people came from Dun Laoghaire. My father won the Victoria Cross. He was very strict but fair. I had four brothers, but they are all dead now. My only family now in Ireland are my nephew and my niece, but they live in the country. I used to love going out – going into town where I was reared. I loved going in and out of the shops ... just looking at things and buying the odd thing. But I can't go out now since the operations on my legs. I loved most going to Mass. That is all over now.

My father died in old age, blessing me because of the way I minded him. When we were young our house was always full of people and full of fun. But old age is not easy. I have only the telly to talk to now. The Vincent de Paul are very good to me. Bernadette and Mary have been my friends for twenty-five years. I look forward to the social every month and the holiday in Kerdiffstown in July. I always dressed up for the parties there. I loved being a lady - just for a day! The young people were great when we met them in Kerdiffstown. I wish we could meet them more often in between.

Lily Murray,
Raheny, Dublin

I Listen with my Eyes

I listen with my eyes and speak with my hands, who am I?

The most remembered memory of my life was in Hearing school when I was a toddler. It was difficult during those times and hard to follow what the teacher was saying. The teacher knew nothing about my deafness or how to cope with me or it. It might be fair to say the teacher thought I was a difficult child. I was there for one month and due to my deafness, was always left out while hanging around with hearing friends. So I transferred to St Joseph's School for Deaf Boys in Cabra. The school was huge and looked scary to go there. My mother didn't like to leave me there because it was far away from home. In fact, you know what mothers are like with their sons. However, my mother found the nearest school from home called Beechpark. This school is for deaf children. In school the first thing I ever saw in my life was lots of deaf pupils signing with their hands. It is amazing when you see small children speaking through their hands.

School was great fun. There I learned lip reading, speech and deaf education. I picked up sign language words from my deaf friends. It was great to use a sign language as it made me feel relaxed. Access and communication was easier than having spoken conversation. It made me who I am.

At age 13, I went to St Joseph's School for Deaf Boys in Cabra where I did my leaving certificate. It was a very successful result for my family and me. It proved that any deaf person can do it. There is no such thing as can't do it. I went to college, doing an Accounting Technician's course. The biggest disappointment for me was the lack of interpreting services and not enough access to information. These issues have forced some deaf students to go to England or America where there is better access and availability to full time interpreters. In Ireland there is little for deaf people going on to further education, but many deaf students want to stay and live in the Ireland they love.

I have a great social life. I am always out doing some sort of sport activities or meeting some deaf friends in the local pub. I am working for the National Association for Deaf People, currently part-time working as Deaf Tech Officer. My job is providing the right information on special equipment, like smoke alarms. Ever wonder how you wake a deaf person up? Well, I will give you a hint … it vibrates instead of ringing. It is very useful to know about these things.

Presently, I am searching for a new job as either a clerical officer or accounting position. It will be hard for me to find a job and get the chance of an interview because many people are fearful of what they do not know about. It is difficult for me to explain that while I am profoundly deaf my brain works just like everyone else's!!! That is the story of my life.

Oh, by the way, the answer to the question at the beginning is: I am profoundly deaf and use sign language!

Shane Keogh,
Employee of National Association of the Deaf (NAD)

WAKING FROM A NIGHTMARE

My name is Julia and I come from a farming area in the West of Ireland. I grew up in a large family home with five sisters and four brothers. My childhood was happy and my home life stable and loving. I met my future husband, also a farmer, when I was eighteen years old, and got married when I was twenty four and he was twenty nine. Our courtship was non-eventful. He bought me presents, opened doors and was kind and gentle. There was no indication of the violence and abuse that I would endure over the next eleven years. The first abusive and violent incident occurred when we went on our honeymoon. He pushed me up against a wall, held his hands to my throat and told me I was now 'his property'. I was in complete shock, but when he said sorry, that it would not happen again and that he did not know what came over him, I believed him. I did not know then that it would get worse.

In the early years my husband would make up some excuse when he hit me, 'the house was untidy', 'the children were crying' or 'the dinner was not ready'. In the end he did not even bother to make excuses, he just believed he had the right to do it. The turning point came one day when we were out on the farm. He was moving cattle, they refused to go where he wanted and, as usual, he blamed me. He lifted a stick and started after me. I stumbled and fell into a drain. He hit me repeatedly, shouting abuse all the time and then he walked off. It was early January and there was snow on the ground. That night I looked at my bruised body in absolute horror, but what worried me most was my state of mind. I knew I had to get away. The next day I told my sister who, when she got over the shock, told me about the Mayo Women's Refuge Services.

When I left my husband, my family were very supportive to me and for that I will always be grateful. The first year after leaving was a real struggle. Not only had I to deal with my own fragile, emotional state, but also my children's distress and unhappiness. The abuse inflicted on me by my husband was something I got used to. The prejudices and attitudes displayed by some, within agencies, was something I was not prepared for. The court process was an absolute nightmare and something I would never want to encounter again. Also, I was constantly having to prove myself over and over again to one state agency or another. I now fully understand when women say the abuse started all over again. Is it any wonder so many women stay silent!

The ongoing support and help from the Refuge Service was excellent. It really helped me through those very hard times. The Society of St Vincent de Paul gave me support and help in many practical ways. When I needed money they gave me some, when I needed a holiday they arranged it. I can assure you that these acts of kindness were appreciated and will never be forgotten. I am now nearly four years down the road since I left. I have my own home, car and job. The children are settled and happy. I still have days when I feel the sadness of the past. I had great hopes for my marriage, family life and relationship. But I have no regrets about leaving a violent destructive and abusive home situation. It takes time. It takes support and it took a belief in myself.

Julia

The Theory is Easy

Love must be tried and tested and proved. It must be tried as though by fire. And fire burns.

Dorothy Day

In one of his books, Alan Patton tells the following story:
In South Africa, during the rise of apartheid, a black South African approached a white school principal. He wanted the school principal to join him and a group of others in resisting the implementation of apartheid. The principal was reluctant because she feared the consequences. She asked her visitor the reasons for his own involvement in this struggle; surely he knew he might be caught by the police, tortured and even put to death. He told her that he believed when he dies, he will meet God. God will first say, "Welcome" and then ask, "Where are your wounds?" He will reply, "I have none", and then God will ask the most awful of questions, "Was there nothing worth fighting for?" "That is a question I could not bear", replied the visitor.

The fight that we are in, is to put our love into practice. A costly fight. Loving God and loving our neighbour is the theory and it sounds very good. But to love God, we need to know that we are loved by God and that this love can be experienced through our neighbours, through reaching out and meeting others, through putting love into practice. Reaching out is not easy. It can be difficult to go out again in the evening, especially when it is dark, cold and wet, only to be met with more demands on our time and little appreciation for what has already been done. It is painful and difficult to know and be with people who are suffering. It is frustrating to see what is needed to ease their suffering and not be in a position to provide it and know that it is unlikely to be provided by anyone for quite some time. To practise love is to become a little powerless at times, to show more of ourselves than we would like, to know we do not have all the answers, to realise that we all have blind spots that need attention from time to time. These things about us are sometimes revealed through difficult relationships with people; perhaps we encounter Christ through them and are invited by Christ to become more truly human and who we are meant to be.

Dear Lord,
St Thomas touched your wounds and recognised you,
Through the wounds of others and our own pain may we come to know you
and experience your healing presence in the world.
We ask this through Christ our Lord.

Dan O'Connell, C.M,
Parish of the Travelling People, Dublin

She's all I've got

Nineteen per cent of 15-24 year olds in Ireland are unemployed.

There were five of us in our family, three boys and two girls. We lived in a flat. It was a small flat and the three of us had bunk beds in one of the bedrooms. We managed all right until my eldest sister got married and had a child. The 'corpo' had nowhere for her to live so she stayed in my ma's flat, herself, her fellow and her child. That made it very crowded. They took one of the bedrooms and the three of us had to share the other bedroom with our sister.

My father became unemployed when I was ten: he had been laid off work and was too old to get another job, at least that's what they all said. He went for loads of interviews but always got turned down. He got depressed and gave up looking. It was then he started drinking. He was a different person when he was drunk, very violent. I often saw him beat my ma and even we got the beatings many a time. My ma couldn't take it and was always going to the doctor for valium. She was in hospital several times for depression and that was the hardest time, being in the flat alone with my da and him drinking.

I loved school. It was great to get out of the flat. There was loads of space and things to do, books to read and games to play. The teachers were real nice but they often didn't stay long. I missed going on outings with the other kids because we just didn't have the money. So I used to work at weekends in the local supermarket, stacking the shelves; it meant that my ma didn't have to give me money for smokes or to go out, because she didn't have it anyway. It was hard to do the homework though, for there was no space in the flat where you could get peace and quiet. I used to get into awful trouble with the teachers for not having it done. But what could I do? The teacher told me that I would never get my exams and there was no point in me doing my Junior.

So I stopped going to school and I got a full-time job in the supermarket. It wasn't much but my ma found the money very useful, she was always short. I didn't like the job, it was very boring and you had to work very hard but it was better than nothing. I got laid off when the supermarket was taken over, the new owners laid half of us off.

I got depressed myself then, hanging around the flat with nothing to do and not being able to give my ma a few bob. I felt useless, I felt I was a burden on my ma, her feeding me and giving me a few bob for smokes and not being able to give her anything back.

I have a lovely girl-friend, but we can't go out much 'cause we don't have the money. I'd like to be able to bring her to the pictures or out to McDonalds, but it's very seldom that I can do it. I worry about the future. I won't be able to give her a good life or have a nice home or be able to give the kids the things I'd like to be able to buy for them. I just feel I'm no good and she would be better off getting someone who can look after her properly. But I wouldn't like to lose her, she's all I have got.

Why do people not want to share more to give everyone a better chance?

Jason

Do not be afraid, for I have redeemed you. I have called you by name, you are mine.

Isaiah, Ch 43, v 1

As a Traveller, prejudice has walked with me on my path of life, as a child and into my adult life. Forced into my life has been the experience of fear, hurt and pain, because of the ignorance of others. As a child I could not understand why this was so. As I grew, I discovered fear was at its core, a fear that in most cases comes from ignorance of my reality. People have allowed their hearts to become darkened to the truth of our faith, a truth we all exist within.

It is through Christ that we have been given the gift of this faith, the reality of this gift we can choose to understand or not. We have the ability and freedom to truly live in the peace of Christ. When we fail to see the face of Christ reflected in the other, then we have also chosen not to see the face of Christ reflected in ourselves. The barriers that exist within ourselves we have created and it is here that our prejudices are at home.

The key to unlocking our prejudice is to see beneath our fear. To know a person by name is to know their reality - too easy do we forget that we are a redeemed people. Traveller and Settled are equally the children of God. I have found the truth of who I am within the words of my God and in finding my own truth, I have found the truth of others. In seeking your reality in God you discover the reality of all.

For I am Yahweh, your God, the holy one of Israel, your saviour. I have given Egypt for your ransom, Cush and Seba in exchange for you. Since I regard you as precious, since you are honoured and I love you.

Isaiah, Ch 43, v 3-4

Lord Christ,
At times we are like strangers on this earth,
disconcerted by all the violence and harsh oppositions.
Like a gentle breeze, you breathe upon us the Spirit of peace.
Transfigure the deserts of our doubts and so prepare us to be bearers
Of reconciliation wherever you place us,
Until a hope of peace arises in our world.

Brother Roger of Taize

Cathleen McDonagh, Theology Student,
All Hallows College, Dublin

Sarajevo

Nobody can destroy soul, the spirit of art and creativity ....

At the beginning of the Second World War, Hitler burned books. Today's fascists are worse and more dangerous, burning not only the books, but the magnificent library building as well. Parallel with their genocide of Muslim and Catholic citizens of Bosnia and Hercegovina, fascist monsters, with their strong, heavy weapons, and God only knows what madness, carried out an evil campaign of 'Urbicide' - the deliberate and systematic destruction of mosques, cathedrals, hospitals, theatres, schools, cultural institutions, museums, concert halls and all communication systems. Of all that was sacred and beautiful, nothing was spared. In August 1992, it was the turn of the National and University Library, that celebrated and historic building, time honoured symbol of Sarajevo itself and of the cultural, ethnic and religious pluralism in our country.

On that terrible summer day, I was in a bomb shelter which was the base for Sarajevo's 'War Theatre', rehearsing our first war play called 'Bomb Shelter'. The whole town was under fire, shelling heavier than usual. Our own building was shaking. Somehow, news reached us that the National Library was burning.

Our immediate reaction was that we must go there. It was absolute madness to even think of going out, but hard as people tried, there was no stopping us. We ran through the rain of shelling towards the National Library as if going about the most innocent of children's games, and straight into the blazing building. We hauled out books in metal cases and cardboard boxes, which we loaded on to the vehicle of a volunteer, saving what we could. The fire brigade tried, but it was impossible to save the beloved building.

During this action two firemen were killed by snipers, but miraculously all the artistic team and technical crew of 'War Theatre' returned safely to the shelter, shocked and disbelieving. I returned to the ruin two days after the fire. The atmosphere was extraordinary, strong and powerful, sacred as a temple, at the same time so sad and glorious. It felt as if the outraged souls of all the authors of the burned books were there in silent warning witness to the world, and the spirits of all the painters, dead and alive.

How is it possible they have destroyed the National Library? How can this happen in a world enjoying unprecedented technological progress? How have we become such victims of our own progress, allowing it to diminish and dehumanise rather than enhance us? Is it correct to call technological and material developments 'progress' which result in such widespread alienation, disintegration? Alienation which leaves people desperately seeking to escape the present and find their humanity, for example, through drugs - and whose vulnerability is so ruthlessly exploited. We have become totally skewed, eclipsed around megalomania.

Now approaching a new century and a new millennium, I worry about the human race and the damage we will continue to do in the name of 'progress'.

I worry. I am afraid. Are you?
It is not enough just to pray, to whatever God, for a better future.
It is necessary that we take urgent, healthy action to return ourselves to the beauty of a life without fear.

Vedran Smailovic, The 'Cellist of Sarajevo',
Co-writer Frances McDonnell

I believe that all people who are homeless are a displaced people.
They have lost their place in our world as it is organised with streets,
houses and addresses. They live in a sort of 'no-man's land',
a bleak territory with no addresses, just endless confusion,
rejection and pain.

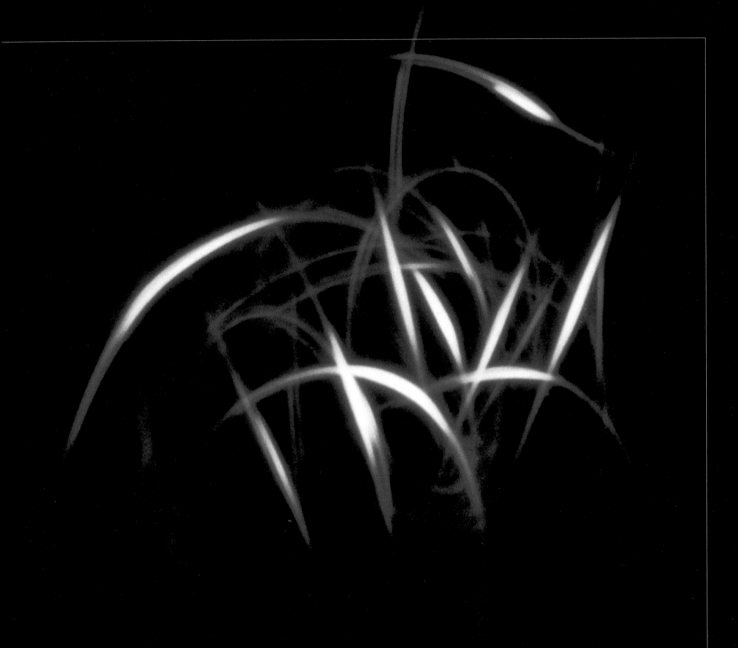

GROUPS

A Displaced People

If home is ... one of the great personal collective works of art that all humans spend their lives attempting to raise up and keep from falling down, then the art of creating homes as distinct from building houses, still has a long way to go, and still remains within the province of magic.

Theodore Zeldin, English historian and anthropologist

Shelter may be the first constituent of a home, but it is not the only one. It is not enough to give a person shelter and a bed for the night, in order to deal with their homelessness; giving them a bed that they can count on again the next night and the next night, is a step in the right direction, but it is still not enough if you are not providing them with a home. People need shelter, but they also need security, love, warmth and above all, to belong - in short, they need a place to call home.

I believe that all people who are homeless are a displaced people. They have lost their place in our world as it is organised with streets, houses and addresses. They live in a sort of 'no-man's land', a bleak territory with no addresses, just endless confusion, rejection and pain.

Our immigrants and asylum seekers are particularly visible as groups of displaced people in our midst today. They can stand, in a way, if we are prepared to face their pain and look them in the eye, for all those we displace and reject, perhaps unobtrusively, such as our own homeless people; our addicts; our travellers; the people we have hidden away in mental hospitals, prisons, emergency shelters; people living with AIDS; all who are ostracised and displaced and considered society's undesirables and unwanted people.

It is my experience that a typical homeless person does not exist. They are all unique and their experience of home and homelessness is also unique. What unites them is their homelessness, the appalling lack of sufficient, suitable, emergency supports, services, accommodation, and the non-availability of accessible, appropriate, affordable, good quality housing. Above all, it is their common humanity that unites them and their desire for a place to call home, which is the deepest desire in every human heart and perhaps the least recognised.

Great Spirit, Spirit of Wisdom and Understanding, be with us on our life journey as we journey with people who are homeless. Guide us as we search to find a home with and for others. Help us to find a home in our own hearts, in the hearts of others and the heart of our God. The journey home for all of us is different, longer or shorter, physically, socially, emotionally, spiritually, but for each of us, it is a journey from home to home.

Sr Stanislaus Kennedy, Director,
Focus Ireland

Just a Second

Every gun that is made, every warship launched, every rocket fired signifies, in the final analysis, a theft from those who hunger and are not fed, those who are cold and are not clothed.

There is much talk about decommissioning of paramilitary weapons in Ireland. This is based on the experience of thirty years of conflict when republican and loyalist paramilitaries were involved in a war with each other and with the State, in which an array of weapons were used by all sides to inflict death and injury on others. Many people argue, however, that decommissioning should go hand in hand with demilitarisation - in other words that all weapons held by all sides should be taken out of the equation.

It is said, for example, that the IRA, one of the groups in the conflict, have a hundred tonnes of weapons and explosives. This is a lot - but it is only a drop in the ocean when you consider that governments around the world spend billions adding to their already huge stockpiles of weapons.

For example, since 1945, thirty to thirty five trillion dollars has been spent on the global arms trade. At the same time, there have been approximately one hundred and fifty wars causing more than twenty-three million deaths. In the last twenty years the number of war refugees has increased from three million to fifteen million. Many conflicts have been made worse by an endless supply of arms, often coming from Europe and the United States. The US alone spends eight hundred million dollars daily on the military. At the same time, eight hundred million people live and die in absolute poverty in Asia and Africa.

The industrialised world as a whole spends more in providing and buying weapons each year than developing countries spend annually on the education of eight hundred million children.
Indeed, there is an urgent need to decommission all weapons in a world which is bursting at the seams with armaments.

Think about eight hundred million. It is a significant figure.
It is the amount of money spent by the United States every day on weapons.
It is the number of people who live and die in absolute poverty in Asia and Africa.
It is the number of children whose education is affected by lack of resources in developing countries.

Imagine what could happen if the money wasted on weapons was used to feed, clothe and educate the poorest people in our world! Why is this not happening? Who decides how the world's limited resources are used? Who benefits? Who loses out?

One of the projects organised by AFRI in recent years was called 'Just a second'. This involved raising the equivalent of what is spent on the arms trade every second (£16,500). We then used this money to fund twenty-six projects in Ireland, Peru, Kenya, Mauritius, Iraq, Sierra Leone, Brazil, Pakistan, Chernobyl, Haiti, El Salvador and India.

This shows how we can choose to use the earth's resources to create instruments of life rather than instruments of death.

Archbishop Tutu sums up the obscenity of the Arms Trade as follows:
"Nations spend obscenely large amounts of public funds on instruments of death and destruction. We know that a very minute fraction of that budget of death would ensure that God's children everywhere would have a clean supply of water, would have enough to eat, would have a reasonable chance of survival. The world will know no peace until there is disarmament and justice."

Joe Murray,
Action From Ireland (AFRI)

The Least, the Last and the Lost

Pope John Paul II, when addressing the Irish Hierarchy in Cabra in 1979, said:

Among those most needing pastoral care from Bishops are prisoners. My dear brothers, do not neglect to provide for their material conditions and their families. Have a special care for young offenders.
So often their wayward lives are due more to society's neglect than to their sinfulness.
Detention should be especially for them a school of rehabilitation.

Twenty years on, the challenge has not changed. As we enter the new millennium how are we going to care for those who are thought of as the Least, the Last and the Lost?

Our prisons are full of people who are psychologically inadequate, financially poor, socially disadvantaged, poorly educated, drug and alcohol addicted and unemployable - society's social rejects. In addition, many of our women prisoners are more sinned against than sinful.

Why do we as a society continue to support and sustain the housing conditions (ghettos) which clearly contribute to juvenile delinquency, drug addiction and the consequential human suffering? Indeed, why do we imprison so many of our poor?

In the Old Testament people looked forward to a God "who would not cherish anger but would delight in showing mercy". We too must show mercy. Most of us claim to be Christians - one of the most basic requirements of Christianity is to forgive those who have offended us.

John Lonergan,
Governor, Mountjoy Prison

Hopes and Dreams

We, as people with disabilities, are shouldering our responsibility to ensure that disabled people are "included" as full citizens in Ireland. It is now time that everyone else joins this process, so that we can all live and participate together as equal members of society.

DFI - What is it?

The Disability Federation of Ireland is a national umbrella organisation for voluntary/non-statutory agencies who provide support services to people with disabilities and disabling conditions. DFI currently has over seventy full member organisations and an association with up to two hundred other organisations throughout its eight regional networks in Ireland.

The role of DFI is to provide a range of supports and services to voluntary organisations that will enable them to deliver the best possible range of services to people with disabilities. Underpinning the activities of each member organisation is the right of people with disabilities to full and equal citizenship.

"People with disabilities do not want to be pitied, nor do they want their disabilities to be dismissed as of little importance. All that is required is a little respect and basic needs and rights. Surely this is not too much to ask?"

"It appears to us that the parents of a disabled child face a lifetime of fighting each and every agency and department for their rights and those of their child."

"I have never had paid work and feel sometimes bitter that I have nothing to show for myself. Even though I don't consider myself old, the years are slipping away in terms of finding a job, like so-called normal people. I have hopes and dreams about the future and don't see why I, or any person with a disability, should have to settle for anything less. I feel if nothing is done that I will still be doing courses to fill in time in ten years time."

The above excerpts are from submissions to The Report of the Commission on the Status of People with Disabilities, *A Strategy for Equality*.

Why aren't people with disabilities getting more jobs in a thriving and prosperous Ireland?
What extra benefits would accrue to us as a nation if they did?

Mary Swanton,
The Disability Federation of Ireland

WHEN THE SAFE PLACE BECOMES A PRISON

Abuse means having your home wrecked, being punched and kicked around the place, having that going on all the whole night, him acting like a lunatic, locking you up. It means verbal abuse, sexual abuse, physical abuse. The television being thrown at you, chairs being smashed over your head, your arm being broken.

Eileen

Abuse always meant to me someone being beaten, but now I realise it's much more than that. It can mean sexual abuse and it can mean mental abuse where your whole self esteem is ripped up. I was never good enough. I was stupid, ugly, too fat, dirty. I was inadequate in every way. You were all the time waiting, waiting for something to happen. I didn't class it as abuse. I just thought I had a bad marriage. We were nearly married seven years before I realised I was an abused woman.

Carrie

Violence against women violates women's human rights. Violence against women in the home is a particularly complex form of violence because the perpetrator of the violence and the victim of the violence live together in the same home. The perpetrator of the violence is usually a partner. It is a grave social problem which threatens the safety, equality and bodily integrity of every woman. Violence against women in the home is a feature of contemporary family life. Irish research shows that eighteen per cent of women reported that they had been subjected at some time to either mental, physical or sexual violence. Many women experienced multiple forms of violence.

For most of us, our homes are a haven from the world. A place to retreat to when life is hard. Most of us treasure the peace and safety, as well as the freedom we have to be ourselves in our own homes. For women and children who are being abused in their own home, that safe place becomes a prison, a place of fear, hurt and pain.

Imagine the constant fear and intimidation, the constant attempts at appeasement in order to avoid a violence that is unavoidable. Imagine the psychological effects of living and often sharing a bed with the person who is persistently committing crimes against your person and your property.

Where do you go when your safe place becomes the most dangerous place you could be?

Many myths and stereotypes exist around domestic violence and around the women who experience battering and/or abuse in their own homes. Most of these myths blame women for the violence which is perpetrated against them. Most of them trivialise the seriousness and the effects of the experience. Women can never be free of either the threat or the experience of violence until social and cultural attitudes to women and women's place in society are challenged by all of us.

We all have a part to play.

Denise Charlton,
Director,
Women's Aid

New Demons

All animals are equal but some animals are more equal than others.

George Orwell

Our contemporary Irish society has developed many positive features consistent with a more open community - we have banished many of the intolerant attitudes of the past which prevented many people from expressing themselves as full human beings. However, some new demons have come to haunt us - an ethos of greed being more important than need has become evident in our approach to the socially and economically deprived in our society.

In the case of Farmers in Poverty, the concept of poverty is wider than just a case of inadequate income. However, in the case of farm families, there is a constant conflict between the financial need of the household and the financial needs of the farm. When money is in short supply, it is heart-rending to have to make a choice between buying something that the children need and buying something that is needed for the animals. If the option to sell the animals is taken, then the potential for future income is taken away. Selling assets is merely a means of creating greater poverty in the future. The wider concept of poverty at farm level would include loneliness, depression, feelings of inadequacy - all this is reflected in the very high suicide rate among farmers. The statistics on farm poverty are widely accepted - unfortunately, little action has been taken to help poor farming families with children.

Many will say 'the poor we will always have with us, in many cases it is their own fault'. If we continue to live in a divided society, where the gap between the 'haves' and the 'have-nots' becomes unbridgeable, it will become impossible to build a truly human society. In time, the marginalised and the excluded will become such a negative force as to undermine our social structures.

Our approach must be to lift all boats by helping those at the bottom of the pile to develop their humanity and create a caring society. It is in the best interest of us all.

Frank Allen, President,
Irish Creamery Milk Suppliers Association (ICMSA)

Children and Poverty in Ireland

According to the Combat Poverty Agency nearly one third of Irish children live in poverty and this is the second highest level of child poverty in the European Union.

(*Investing in Children* - Submission to the Minister for Social, Community and Family Affairs on the 1999 Budget, Dublin: Combat Poverty Agency, 1998)

We need to be careful about thinking in terms of a 'poor' or a 'rich' child. Children are born into and raised in poor or rich environments. Children behave and develop according as they adapt to and influence these environments. The environments themselves set the boundaries to what children can or cannot do; to what they can or cannot become; and to whether their experiences are repeated by their own children. Ireland, despite its image of Celtic Tiger, now has the second worst environment for supporting children in the European Union.

If we want to change or improve outcomes for children, then we should change those things in their environment that inhibit or restrict their development. We should change the nature of their physical environment so that they have adequate space to play, to be creative and to build social relationships; change their education so that it can fulfil the promise of universal access and equality; change the way in which health and social services are provided so that the child and not the service providers are central; and above all, change the way in which their parents receive income support so that they can sustain a decent family living standard without having to feel demeaned.

Isn't one way of focusing our energies to tackle child poverty to pressurise government to agree a standard of living, including specific references to family income, housing, education and health and to insist that no child be required to live below this standard?

Barry Cullen,
The Children's Research Centre,
Trinity College, Dublin

Pressing the Altar for conviction

Now I live by a famous strand
where seabirds cry in the small hours
like incredible souls
and even the range wall of the promenade
that I press down on for conviction
hardly tempts me to credit it.

Seamus Heaney, In Illo Tempore, *Station Island,*
Faber and Faber 1984

We never had it so good. We never imagined we would live to see such prosperity. And now we know that the rising tide doesn't lift every boat. Beached all around us are those who hadn't the resources to take advantage of the tide. And sometimes we stand between the market and our faith, between where we are and what we believe, the one goading us to run with the opportunity we're offered, the other reminding us about those who may be left behind.

The man was angry. Very angry. Every morning he had to pass a line of Traveller caravans on the side of the road. No water, no electricity, no sanitary accommodation, no heat. The things he saw! The condition of the children. You wouldn't believe it! This would have to stop! It shouldn't be allowed to continue! Righteous anger, you might almost say, but directed at me.

I had suggested somewhere that providing a halting site might be an appropriate response by the local community. The Residents Committee, of which he was a prominent member, had erected a series of signs "No Halting Site here". Would I like THEM to live near me? What if the value of my house diminished? Then some weeks later, it was Christmas. We broke bread together around an altar. We reflected on the text: *She wrapped him in swaddling clothes, and laid him in a manger because there was no room for them at the inn* (Luke, Ch.2, v.7). We received Communion together. We exchanged our certainties.

In Heaney's poem, *In Illo Tempore*, there is a transition from an experience of believing in everything to an experience of believing in nothing. As I felt the altar under my hands, as I pressed down my hands on it for conviction, I felt that he and I might be going through that same transition. And I wondered whether it might be the case that those of us who believe everything can sometimes end up believing in very little, because what we believe has become disjointed from the inn, from the side of the road. Splayed missals. Broader phylacteries. Exotic tassels. Hollow words.

Lord, we believe that everyone is made in your image, that everyone is a brother and a sister to you and us, that everything we have has come from you. Deepen our faith in you and in what you teach us. Help us to make it real in our lives, so that we may respect all our brothers and sisters in your world. Amen.

Fr Brendan Hoban,
Ballyglass,
Enniscrone, Co Sligo

Community and AIDS
(i)

Life breaks us all and afterwards many are strong in the broken places.

Ernest Hemingway

I know a woman who lost a son and her son's partner within the space of one week and who is much afraid because of the very fragile health of two other sons, a daughter and her daughter's child, all of whom are HIV Positive. And I know another woman who within a short few years lost two sons and two daughters. I recall three years ago on a community day out how a nine year old girl, who was orphaned, commented on seeing me messing with my own children that they did not realise how lucky they were. I have spent much time with men and women in their twenties and thirties in their hospital beds and I heard them speak about their fears, about their families and about their God. I am speaking of a community that has had a problem with drugs and a problem with AIDS. My community has lost over seventy young people in recent years from an AIDS related illness - almost all drug related.

There was in our community a short number of years ago a bank. It was positioned in a very prominent place. The bank moved out of our community. A funeral undertaker took over its premises. Most of the young people who have died from AIDS and drug related illnesses have been laid out there. Most parts of Ireland experience drug misuse. Some parts however have drug problems. A community that swaps a bank for a funeral undertaker to bury its young dead speaks of the latter category. Multiple deaths from AIDS related illnesses and a drug related problem are not just accidents. They are much more.

So, what's the story? Do you have one that tells a yet deeper story?
Jesus, help us to take to heart the heart of your story which is "to do justice,
to love mercy and to walk humbly with our God" (Micah, Ch.6, v.8).

Tony MacCarthaigh,
Director, Rialto Community Drugs Team

COMMUNITY AND AIDS
(ii)

Good friends we've had and friends we've lost along the way ...

Bob Marley

For the past six years I have run a home-care programme for people and their families affected by HIV/AIDS 'along the way'. I made friends and 'lost them'... They chose to be my friend - I did not choose them, nor did I choose to lose them. Many are dead - now I have a choice - to remember them.

Do you choose your friends? Are they always like minded, or do you embrace those who choose you?

Some day when I'm lonely wishing you weren't so far away - then I will remember things we said to-day...

Lennon and McCartney

Terri Colman-Black,
AIDS Care Education & Training (ACET), Dublin

No room at the Inn

The Christian Community in Ireland is becoming more conscious of the needs of refugees and asylum seekers. At a time when the number of refugees and asylum seekers arriving at our shores is rising, we need to re-affirm and restate our faith in our mutual brotherhood and sisterhood. The temptation is to define our community in narrow exclusive terms. To do so would be to betray the gospel. As Christians, our community must include the stranger and reach out to the persecuted, the oppressed and the needy outsider.

From the Foreword to *Refugees and Asylum Seekers : A Challenge to Solidarity*

(A Joint Policy Document of the Irish Commission For Justice and Peace and Trócaire, December 1997)

Ireland is entering a new phase in its history. We can choose to turn inwards and reject the stranger and refugee in need, turning our back on our own history in doing so. Or, we can commit ourselves to creating a more welcoming, more inclusive society.

The Jesuit Refugee Service, founded in 1980 by Pedro Arrupe, S.J., Superior General of the Jesuits, expresses its vision in these words:

"We accompany the refugees, we serve their needs, we advocate their cause in an uncaring world."

The Biblical vision of hospitality to the stranger challenges us today in new ways:

"If a stranger lives with you in your land, do not molest him. You must count him as one of your own countrymen and love him as yourselves, for you were once strangers yourselves in Egypt."

(Leviticus, Ch 19, v 33ff).

Frank Sammon S.J., Director,
Jesuit Refugee Service, Ireland

Was Jesus a Capitalist?

And He said to those standing by: 'Take the pound from him and give it to the one who has ten pounds.'
And they said to Him: 'But, Sir, he already has ten pounds.'
I tell you, to everyone who has will be given more; but from the man who has not,
even what he has will be taken away.

Parable of the Talents, Luke, Ch 10

Could Jesus possibly have said that? The Jesus who in the same gospel enunciates the first beatitude "Blessed are the poor". We need to probe its deeper meaning. The context provides the most helpful clue, i.e. the parable of the talents. Jesus is articulating a profound feature of human life: there is no standing still; we go forward or we go backward.

When I work hard at developing a particular talent (e.g. a skill of hand, or foot, or eye or mind) I grow more skilful. A man or woman may have a working knowledge of Irish from school; if they use it frequently, they can become quite fluent. If they never use it, they will forget even the little they know.

Similarly with any area of human giftedness, be it music, song or a spiritual gift of prayer. The man who gives up praying will lose even what he has. He who buries his talent, it has been wittily said, makes a grave mistake. "Even what he has will be taken away."

Let us listen to Rudyard Kipling.

Addressing a class of graduates in Montreal, Canada, he chose the following theme:

If a person's scale of values is based solely on material wealth, that person will be in difficulty all his or her life. "Do not pay too much attention to fame, power and money," he said. "Some day you will meet a person who cares for none of these, and then you will know how poor you are."

A final word to Nelson Mandela on believing in our greatest talent:
Our deepest fear is not that we are inadequate.
It is our light, not our darkness, that most frightens us.
I ask myself: Who am I to be brilliant, talented, famous?
Actually, who are you not to be? You are a child of God.
Your playing small doesn't serve the world.
We were born to make manifest the glory of God that is within us.
It is not just in some of us, it's in everyone.

Nelson Mandela, 1994 Inaugural Speech

Fr. Seamus Ryan,
Parish Priest, Ballyfermot,
Dublin

A SECOND CHANCE

The worst thing I ever did was leaving school and not finishing my education, and especially not doing my Junior Cert. Even if I would of gotten that, it wouldn't have been too bad. But my parents split up and I then had to be the responsible one. I had to go and get money for my Ma and that was the reason for my leaving school.

Jason, aged sixteen years, St Vincent's Trust

The issue is quite simple that, contrary to what we hold to be among the most important building blocks in modern day Ireland, not all young people have an equal opportunity for education. I have worked for St Vincent's Trust for nearly ten years: its aim is to empower the most vulnerable young people, who are marginalised in this way by society, to realise their full potential by offering them a second chance.

We welcome a broad spectrum of young men and women but they are generally from poor backgrounds and have experienced abuse in many forms, inadequate parenting, absent parents, conflict and violence at home and sexual abuse. They have often been drawn into substance abuse and its accompanying life of petty crime. Most of them have left school before fifteen years of age and therefore, not only have poor literacy and numeracy skills, but have no formal qualifications either. Many are already known to the various branches of the helping agencies and the police.

Let me give you just a few facts and figures about Ireland in the nineties: about four thousand young people leave second level school each year with no qualification at all; an additional one thousand do not even progress to second level school; eight thousand leave school having completed the Junior Certificate only; over five thousand leave school without achieving five passes in the Leaving Certificate examination.

It is the poor who suffer from educational disadvantage; they live in those situations where the cycle of poverty is most difficult to break, most often, but not wholly in urban inner-city areas. Educational disadvantage is, of its nature, a root cause of poverty and exclusion.

Our mission and charisma is in the Vincentian tradition and must therefore evoke our sense of compassion and commitment. It can be encapsulated in the words of St Vincent to Sr Jeanne: "It is only because of your love ... because of your love alone ... that the Poor will forgive you for the bread you give them." At St Vincent's Trust we are convinced of the value of this work because each time that we create an opportunity for one young person to begin again, we offer that young man or woman an opportunity to break through that cycle or the iniquitous trap of poverty.

The essential key to this is the building of good relationships in an atmosphere of trust. I never cease to be excited when we enable even just one other person to engage in the work of their own transformation. However, the critical challenge, the challenge of the gospel, is to stand alongside the young people, not just to help them, but to allow ourselves to be drawn into our own process of change and growth with all its necessary pain and struggle.

What mind set, preconceptions and prejudices, do I bring to this reality?
How do I view and value those caught in the trap of Educational Disadvantage?

Christ said, "I came that they may have life and have it abundantly" (John, Ch 10, v 10).
How can I individually, and we together, contribute to the work of justice,
transformation and liberation in this context in order that we might fulfil His wish?

Sr Catherine Prendergast,
Director, St Vincent's Trust,
Henrietta Street Dublin

Bombed and Forgotten

I think our politicians have kicked us in the teeth. We can't lay our loved ones to rest until we know the truth and we get answers. We want to know why this happened. We want to know why there wasn't more done. When these people were killed we were handed a life sentence. It's something we have to live with every day of our lives.

Michelle O'Brien
(whose mother was killed in the Dublin bombings in 1974 when she was only eight years old)

Thirty-three people were killed in the Dublin-Monaghan bombings. The political response to the inchoate tragedy was a moral test which those in power in 1974 failed miserably. While the intervening years have provided ample opportunities to redress the situation, despite a lot of lip service from all parties when in opposition, successive governments have sat on their hands. After a few weeks it was swept under the carpet and it was just forgotten. All the other atrocities like Enniskillen, Warrington and Bloody Sunday are often spoken of, and rightly so, but even southern politicians never mention the Dublin-Monaghan bombings. That hurts a lot of people.

Death always sends a chill through the bones. Each death is a painful reminder of the ultimate and unwelcome end for us all. It is all the more harrowing when thirty-three people are cut down brutally in the prime of their lives. Yet, for their loved ones left behind, the tragedy is magnified by the fact that these people who were robbed of dignity in life are now being denied dignity in death. In the words of a father of one of the people who died: 'We've been treated like lepers. Nobody in authority wants to know about us.' What must it be like to be a forgotten victim?

Lord, may your spirit live within me, showing me to love as you love,
teaching me to care for all your children, regardless of their appearance or status.

John Scally
Author.

The Risk Factor is Being Female

'This is not random violence ... the risk factor is being female'.

Lori Heise, U.S.A

We talk about 'domestic violence' or 'family violence' but in the majority of cases it is not 'the family'. The fact is, in most cases violence against women and children happens in the home and is perpetrated by men known to them. The violence is premeditated and designed to humiliate, threaten and control. As a society we need to challenge the habits, beliefs and traditions which permit some men to assume that the abuse of women is an acceptable option for them. Male violence needs to be viewed in a wider social context rather than as an individual problem between two people. Communities have a collective responsibility to condemn such violence as it will only stop when men stop being violent and society stops condoning it.

On the day when it will be possible for woman to love not in her weakness but in her strength, not to escape herself but to find herself, not to abase herself but to assert herself - on that day love will become for her, as for man, a source of life and not of mortal danger.

Simone de Beauvoir

Victims are chosen because of their gender. The message is domination: Stay in your place or be afraid. Contrary to the argument that such violence is only personal or cultural, it is profoundly political. It results from the structural relationships of power, domination and privilege between men and women in society. Violence against women is central to maintaining those political relations at home, at work, and in all public spheres.

Charlotte Bunch

Josephine McGourty,
Director,
Mayo Women's Refuge & Support Services

Travellers and Discrimination

Any religion concerned about the souls of people and not concerned with the slums that damn them, the economics that strangle them and the social conditions that imprison them is a molly coddle religion awaiting burial.

Martin Luther King

When we call Travellers offensive names, to their face or behind their back, when we refuse them access to ordinary everyday services, such as hairdressers, pubs, laundries, cinemas and shops - purely on the basis of being born a Traveller, then we discriminate against these men and women. When our schools do not reflect their distinct culture, when we refuse to provide decent accommodation, exclude them from employment and continue to allow an infant mortality rate three times higher than that of the settled community, on the basis of their ethnic identity - then in a more structured and organised way, we continue to discriminate against them. As a group they are systematically excluded from local parishes and communities and are marginalised within society. They are the 'other' in Ireland today. They are feared and discrimination is an expression of our fear.

'The Christian Community welcomes you with great joy' are the first words spoken on behalf of the church - the people of God - to any child being baptised. However, these words have a hollow and empty ring to them when a Traveller child is brought to this 'sacrament of belonging'. For this child and for their brothers and sisters, father, mother and all their family, welcome is not what is offered. Rather, a life as objects of fear and hostility and the experience of an all-encompassing exclusion is given instead. Discrimination is corrosive, being told that you are not equal nor deserving of respect and that you are somehow 'less' than others, is felt very deeply and has a profound impact on the life of the Traveller community. This reality mocks our religious practice and flies in the face of God, whose vision, as revealed through Jesus, was that peace and justice, love and compassion, holiness and fullness of life for all might be realised. Each of us needs to take account and ask ourselves about our place and responsibility in the continued exclusion of Travellers in Ireland today. What can I/we do now?

God of life, intimacy and passion;
help us to recognise your healing presence in the world.
To see it in the dignity and humanity of those on the margins
and in the very bones of one another.
To know it in trust, in friendship and in forgiveness,
to see it in the dangerous and costly step of opening ourselves to the 'other'.
Help us to reach out, fear less, value diversity and help us to be free.
We ask this through Christ our Lord.

Dan O'Connell, C.M.,
Parish of the Travelling People, Dublin

Wailing at the wall of Officialdom

...Smug, smiling, filing cabinet face
closed to my unspoken entreaty,
social justice is my right,
don't dole it out like charity ...

This is an extract from a poem which was written by me in the early eighties during a time when I and my five children experienced the steady, daily drip of indignity and the erosion of our hopes, energy and spirit, due to poverty. Included in the poem was the line:

...today I wailed at the wall of officialdom,
and my mind screamed a slow sad caoin for the 'us',
and damned their social welfare.

Twelve years later women are still wailing at the wall of officialdom; new statistics are available which reveal that women and children are still living in poverty. In a major study of poverty in the 1990s, the results revealed that the numbers of people experiencing poverty since 1987 has risen.

Since 1987, the risk of poverty has increased for households headed by women, single adult households, and the elderly - children also continue to face a higher risk of poverty than adults.

Is this the Ireland that you and I want to bring into the millennium? Why can't I take comfort from the report which goes on to state ... *however the depth of their poverty has been reduced, the numbers of people experiencing the worst levels of poverty has been reduced ...*

One of the key challenges facing us is the way in which we measure poverty in absolute terms. It insults people who are poor in the midst of a booming economy. It insults their cultural, political, emotional and social needs. It makes the managing of poverty doubly difficult for women. Let us remember that women have been managing poverty for decades in Ireland. Women and children are still being destroyed by poverty and deprivation, whilst all around, people are living in full and plenty.

We can no longer stand aside and be part of the problem. We need to be part of the solution. Philanthropy and charity won't cure poverty. Only a radical, very radical anti-poverty campaign will. The elimination of poverty and the creation of a just society must be placed at the top of the national agenda in Ireland. All of us must take responsibility to promote change and to support agents for justice.

Have we got the moral courage to take up this challenge? I hope so, for all our sakes. An unequal society such as ours, is a deep outrage in a burgeoning economy and it's time for it to stop. The time is NOW for us to cry STOP to our badly divided society.

Cathleen O'Neill,
Community Development Worker

A Drain on Society's Resources

Now suppose a man comes into your synagogue, well dressed and with a gold ring on, and at the same time a poor man comes in, in shabby clothes and you take notice of the well dressed man and say: 'Come this way to the best seats'; then you tell the poor man, 'Stand over there' or 'You can sit on the floor by my foot-rest'.

In making this distinction among yourselves have you not used a corrupt standard? Listen, my dear brothers: it was those who were poor according to the world that God chose to be rich in faith and to be the heirs to the kingdom which he promised to those who love him. You, on the other hand, have dishonoured the poor.

James, Ch 2, v2-6

Poverty means lurching from one financial crisis to another: children's birthdays, first communion, confirmation, ESB bills, kitchen appliances (bought second hand) breaking down, a seemingly endless succession of crises, stress, borrowing and more stress. And then there is Christmas! So many parents, even the children sometimes, tell me that they would like to fall asleep three weeks before Christmas and wake up in the New Year. Christmas is not the joyful celebration of the birth of Jesus, it is a financial crisis which may take the whole year to recover from.

Eleven per cent of Irish people are below the poverty line (as defined in the United Nations Human Development Report 1998). Among seventeen industrial countries, those with the highest incidence of poverty are the United States, followed by Ireland and the United Kingdom.

What is the hardest thing about being poor? Is it sometimes being hungry? Is it being dressed in poor clothes? Is it not being able to take part in activities and events that cost money, like your friends do? No. Is it the constant stress and hassle worrying how the bills are going to be paid, worrying how you are going to cope? Yes and No.

The hardest thing about being poor is to feel that nobody cares, that you are of little value, of no importance, that you do not count, that you are different. It is to be made feel that you are not wanted, that you are a drain on society's resources, that you are unreliable and suspect. It is to feel that your dignity is not respected, that you are a second class citizen in your own country, that society often feels it would be better off if you did not exist. The hardest thing about being poor is that you are also made to feel inadequate.

If you want to understand why people are poor, you have to analyse how people get rich. Four per cent of the combined wealth of the richest two hundred and twenty-five people in the world would provide basic education, basic health care, adequate food, safe water and sanitation for every human being in the world and reproductive care for all women.

Peter McVerry S.J.,
Ballymun

LETTERFRACK

Podded in varnished pews, stunted in beds
Of cruciform iron, they bruise with sad, hurt shame:
Orphans with felons, bastards at loggerheads
With waifs, branded for life by a bad name.

(From *The Price of Stone* by Richard Murphy)

I work in a building which, for almost one hundred years, was known as Letterfrack Industrial School. It was built in 1887 for "Roman Catholic Boys" and it closed in 1974. At its peak, it could cater for over one hundred and twenty boys, usually between the ages of six and sixteen years. They were mostly in Richard Murphy's words "orphans, felons or waifs".

Old buildings capture and hold myriad stories. They can be revered or reviled, not just for how they look in the landscape, but for what happens in them. In a time when we are sold the doctored images of buildings, we need to remind ourselves to look beyond the physical structure and acknowledge the spirit, the soul that lives within them. It can reflect who we were or help us create who we want to be.

The local community now owns this building and because of the successful development efforts of the people, it buzzes with activity, energy and creativity. Rooms that were once dormitories, classrooms, workshops, kitchens, refectory and laundry, now house over one hundred and thirty people, most of them young, engaged in building furniture which is useful and beautiful, accessing information in a modern library, using computers or laboratory equipment, running a community radio service, meeting the needs of the elderly, those with learning difficulties or people on low incomes.

In less than one generation, the spirit of the building has been reformed. The old fear of being "sent to Letterfrack" has been replaced by the desire to "get into Letterfrack". Yet, the building still looks much the same as it did fifty or seventy years ago. A place of shame can become a place of pride and hope.

Kieran O'Donohue, Director,
Connemara West

SO CONDEMNED I STAND

And so condemned I stand,
Just an ordinary man
Like thousands beside me in the queue
For as long as I live
I never will forgive
You've stripped me of my dignity and pride
You stripped me bare.
You stripped me bare.

From *Ordinary Man* by Peter Hames

For almost two decades Ireland suffered one of the worst unemployment problems in the developed world: during the 1980s the number of people registered as unemployed doubled from sixty thousand to one hundred and twenty thousand, then doubled again to a quarter of a million. There were eighty thousand fewer people at work at the end of the decade than there were at the start and over a hundred thousand people had emigrated. In the early 1990s, almost one worker in five was jobless.

Despite the widespread view that unemployment affected us all, most of this enormous catastrophe of unemployment was suffered by a minority of people, living in quite easily identifiable areas. Despite the recent growth in jobs, many of these people and their children find it virtually impossible to get back into decent reasonably secure employment. Because jobs are now being created and some employers are having recruitment problems, many people have concluded that the 'jobs famine' is over. Public sympathy is turning against unemployed people, and there is a growing impatience and resentment about the number of people who remain unemployed. Because there are some jobs around, are we beginning to conclude that the unemployed can have no one to blame for their problems but themselves?

"Ordinary Man" (written by Peter Hames and sung by Christy Moore) is, extraordinarily, one of the few popular songs or poems which deals with the appalling experience which so many people went through over the last twenty years. For that reason it might appear an uninspired choice, even a cliché. But it is worth looking again at this particular verse. The unemployed man declares that he "never will forgive" those who took away his "dignity and pride". He is direct in his accusation, blaming "You" who have done this to him. Hundreds of thousands of ordinary men and women have sung along to these words of irredeemable bitterness. They have recognised the humiliation which goes with being "stripped bare" of dignity in front of your children, family and community.

Yet, only a few years later, the part of society which did not suffer this destruction looks at those who did and expects them to simply pick themselves up. It expects them to be able to walk into the first job offer that comes along, just as if nothing has happened.

How did ordinary men and women survive the humiliation and despair of mass unemployment? How did they reconcile themselves to a society which told them they were of no worth and that they would never work again? And finally, to ask ourselves how people and communities who have been through this can adjust to a society that is now newly rich and self-satisfied, yet still offers them so little.

What does Irish society need to do to earn the forgiveness of those who were so utterly pushed to the side during the fourteen years of the jobs famine?

If it is 'pay back time' in Ireland, to whom is the debt really owed?

Mike Allen,
General Secretary,
Irish National Organisation For the Unemployed (INOU)

*It is time we realised that if we develop
zero tolerance on poverty
there will be little need for zero
tolerance on crime.*

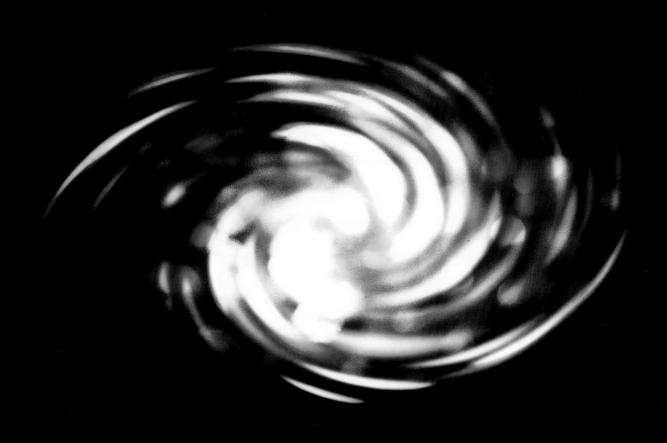

UNEQUAL SOCIETY

EQUALITY OF OPPORTUNITY

At an early age I took my mind to this question of the ages - why are the many poor?

Jim Larkin (1919)

Statistical evidence in relation to urban poverty, early school leaving, drug taking, and drug related crime, tells us that the condition of many deprived urban areas appears to be growing worse. Much of the data portrays a vivid picture of a specific type of poverty and deprivation which is largely confined to pockets of urban local authority housing.

The picture is of a type of poverty where the local populations are vulnerable and disadvantaged on many counts, but most alarming of all, they are extremely vulnerable to drug misuse.

It is evident that a large proportion of crime has socio-economic roots. Statistics show us that in 1996, fifty-six per cent of the Mountjoy Prison population came from six deprived Dublin communities. It is, nonetheless, clear that the large majority of people living in these deprived areas are honest, decent people who want nothing more than a decent lifestyle for themselves and their children.

Since the State was founded, one of its main objectives has been the relief of poverty and the equalisation of opportunity for all our people. As we approach the new millennium, with national macro-economic indicators more positive than I have ever seen in my lifetime, we must ask why we are not making a better fist of it, in the interests of the people we serve.

Research undertaken as part of the four pilot programmes of the Integrated Services Project (in Dublin and Cork city) strongly suggest that it is not simply an issue of the level of resources, but the way in which they are deployed and co-ordinated, and the extent of community participation in the delivery of services.

We urgently need much closer working relationships between the statutory agencies themselves, based on the clear priority of the real need of the communities in which they are working. Each community must be a full participant in the design, planning, delivery and evaluation of services. The entire hierarchy of needs must be addressed - the environment, housing, health, child care, education, recreation, youth activities, training, employment, community developments.

Delivering change will not be easy.

It never is or never has been. Yet, that is what we must do. And we must do it together, in the people's name.

That we may work hand in hand with our brothers and sisters who through no fault of their own,
live in deprived circumstances, listening respectfully to their wisdom,
building with them a new partnership based on their rights and our obligations,
so that the Irish nation can truly share the richness of its people,
by investing the riches of its resources in them.
We ask you Lord.

Bertie Ahern,
An Taoiseach

The State of the Nation

It is a reproach to religion and government to suffer so much poverty and excess.
William Penn (1644-1718), *Reflections and Maxims*

The greatest of evils and the worst of crimes is poverty.
George Bernard Shaw, *Major Barbara* (1907)

It is an extraordinary paradox that on the one hand we are living through a period of major increases in wealth and affluence, while on the other hand, those on the margins of society are being left further behind and are experiencing real misery and hardship. Furthermore, at a time when it is possible to narrow the divide we are making deliberate choices in the distribution and allocation of resources that will ensure that for many that wide gap will continue.

The most recently available figures show that between twenty and thirty per cent of the population fall below income poverty lines and between nine and fifteen per cent are consistently poor. High levels of educational disadvantage and literacy problems persist. Hospital and housing waiting lists are growing. Minority groups like Travellers and Refugees experience discrimination and exclusion. Long-term unemployment figures remain high. The problems of urban blackspots or peripheral rural communities persist. The problems of drugs and crime bedevil many disadvantaged communities. For many, key services such as transport, recreation and culture remain difficult to access and of poor quality. Nor will all this fade away. The most shocking thing is that children face a greater risk of poverty than adults. The cycle is set to repeat itself. Growing up in poverty will mean that many children will experience poor health, will do less well at school and will be at greater risk of being involved in crime and anti-social behaviour. Their talents and potential will be underdeveloped.

How is it as a society that we can allow such inequality and injustice to persist? Why, as we become more affluent, do some of us seem to become less tolerant and begin to blame the victims of poverty or to discriminate against anyone who seems different? Why do others slip into a culture of contentment, complacently assuming that because they are all right, everyone else must be the same, thus conveniently ignoring the misery around them? We are a society in transition. We are at a cross roads. We do have a choice.

We can continue to complacently believe that the market place can solve everything and to pursue rampant individualism and personal gain - in my view a recipe for persistent deep-seated inequality and poverty. Alternatively, we can recognise that a fair and just society is built on the recognition of the interdependence of all and reassert our belief in the dignity of all people and their rights to participate fully in the life of the society in which they live. This is not a question of charity but of justice. It is also a question of common sense and economic prudence. It is only by investing our new wealth in addressing the underlying causes of poverty that in the long-term we can ensure a stable society and continued economic success.

If a house divided against itself cannot stand (Matthew, Ch 3, v 25)
then can a nation divided against itself survive? How can we move from a divided to an inclusive society?

Hugh Frazer, Director,
Combat Poverty Agency (CPA)

Can one person make a difference?

We believe apartheid is a crime. What we are doing is an act of solidarity with the black people of South Africa. People say we should be glad to have a job but this is a moral issue.

Mary Manning

If one were to try to imagine a person least in a position to make a difference to an international issue occurring five thousand miles away, a young woman operating a cash register in a supermarket would surely figure as an unlikely candidate. Yet this is what happened in the case of Mary Manning.

On 19 July, 1984, Mary Manning, a shop assistant in Dunnes Stores in Henry Street, Dublin, decided that she would no longer handle or check out fruit imported from South Africa. Mary, then aged twenty-one years, decided to take a stand against the evil of apartheid, in solidarity with black workers in South Africa. Mary was suspended by Dunnes Stores for refusing to handle 'the fruits of apartheid' and was immediately joined on the picket line by nine of her co-workers. The rest of the story is about the domino effect of Mary's action.

In what one commentator described as 'the most unique dispute in Irish Trade Union history', the picket became a conduit and a catalyst for Irish anti-apartheid action and revulsion. Mary and her colleagues were joined on the picket lines by members of the Irish public from all walks of life. The Irish Trade Union movement, the Congregation of Religious in Ireland, as well as solidarity groups such as AFRI and the media, gave them strong support. In South Africa, the ANC, the South African Congress of Trade Unions and the South African Council of Churches gave huge publicity to the picket and voiced much gratitude to the young Irish protesters.

This strike, which was more than the usual industrial dispute between workers and management, dragged on into its second year, with much suffering for the workers and their families. The dispute was also an embarrassment to the Irish government which continued to sit on the fence, saying it was in favour of economic sanctions against South Africa but refusing to implement any. However, after much pressure from the Irish public, the media, and especially the Nobel Peace prize winner, Archbishop Desmond Tutu, the Irish government decided to ban the importation of all South African fruit and vegetables. This allowed Mary and her colleagues to return to work.

So ended the Dunnes Stores Workers protest against apartheid. One person, Mary Manning, had made a huge difference.

What pressures were on Mary Manning and her fellow workers during the two year protest ?

Joe Murray,
Action from Ireland (AFRI)

Destroying our Home

Christians, in particular, realise that their responsibility within creation and their duty towards nature and the Creator are an essential part of their faith.

Pope John Paul II wrote these insightful words in a document called *Peace With God the Creator, Peace with All Creation*. The Pope was attempting to alert Catholics to the extensive damage that was being wreaked on specific eco-systems, like rain forests and on the global environment as a whole.

He called attention to the problem of global warming. This is a direct result of the wasteful way people in First World countries have burned fossil fuel for decades. We know now that global warming will raise sea levels and intensify tropical storms. Unfortunately, the main victims of such climate change will be poor people living in low lying countries like Egypt and Bangladesh.

The rampant destruction of tropical forests has led to the extinction of tens of thousands of species. This wanton destruction of life is an insult to the Creator. Our misuse of chemicals like CFCs has led to the thinning of the ozone layer which screens out the ultra violet rays of the sun. As a result, we are already experiencing a significant rise in skin cancer. Finally, as we reflect on the waters of the world during the International Year of the Oceans (1998), we have come to realise that pollution of the oceans is at crisis point.

It is obvious that our present way of living is unsustainable. Unless we change our behaviour we will pass on an ugly and run down planet to future generations. To avoid creating a hell on earth, each one of us must begin to live more simply, avoiding waste wherever possible. Political will is needed to promote environmental policies at local, national and international level, designed to halt the present destruction and aimed at healing the damage already done. As Christians, we need to gather our energies and to see caring for the earth as central to our Christian vocation.

God, Our Creator, you have given us the Earth, the sky, the rivers and the seas. Show us the way to care for the Earth, not just for today, but for future generations. Let no plan of ours damage or destroy the beauty of your creation. Send forth your Spirit to direct us to care for the Earth.

Sean McDonagh,
Society of St Columban,
Navan

Soulwork and Inclusion

I am of the family of the universe, and with all of us together, I do not fear being alone; I can reach out and touch a rock or a hand or dip my feet in water. Always there is somebody close by and when I speak I am answered by the plane's roar or the bird's whistling or the voices of others in conversation far apart from me. When I lie down to sleep, I am in the company of the dark and the stars ... Sun and moon, I smile at you both and spread my arms in affection and lay myself down at full length for the earth to know I love it too and am never to be separated from it.

David Ignatow, *Earth Prayers*

Inclusion begins with each of us. To be inclusive we need to bring all our capacities and aspects fully and freely into our daily round. We create space for this inclusion of more of ourselves by giving less significance and time to rational, linear and one-dimensional ways of thinking and living.

The free space is given to our intuition, our stories, our play and creativity, our capacity for silence, for wonder, for at-oneness with nature, a revelling in our senses, our physicality and sensuality, our attunement to the cycles of the days, the months, the years.

Take a moment to reflect ... how much time in any day or week is given to moving all of yourself into your life... listening to the wisdom of your dreams and hearing what your body is telling you? ...how much time is spent listening to your inner stories, staying with the truthfulness of your senses, spending time with nature, attuning yourself to the cycles of the moon, the energies of the seasons, the presence of nature? ... and how much goes into activity that excludes so much of the mystery of who you are and your interconnection with all that is?

How can we allow others to have their rightful space and place when we have no sense of such a place? How can we include an aspect of another that we have excluded and denied in ourselves?

As a new-born babe I crawl from my mother's womb
And stand on wobbly legs in the new world,
Wash the new body that has just been
So tenderly born from a lifetime of labour,
And walk to stand before the fire.
I raise my face to your infinite sky
And feel your touch of grace.
Your gentle raindrops kissing my skin,
Your singing wind that moves the trees,
The hot breath of your dancing fire,
Your wet, rich earth beneath my feet.
O Spirit, I recognise you now: My father, my mother, my unseen lover -
You've been here always in all things; In all things has your spirit lived for me;
From all things has your spirit loved me.
Through all things has your spirit touched me. And never was I left alone, nor could I be
In this truer world of holy people and living stone.

Rochelle Wallace, *Earth Prayers*

Soulwork births us into "this truer world of holy people and living stone".

Eleanor McClorey,
Development Worker,
Community Action Network (CAN)

SPORT AS UNIFIER

The scientific nature of the ordinary man, is to go on out and do the best he can.

John Prine, USA Singer/Songwriter

Both of us have been sports fanatics all our lives, but particularly football. Since Easter 1997, through managing and coaching Republic of Ireland underage teams, we have played fifty international games. During this period we have competed against teams from various parts of the world - China, Ghana, Argentina, Azerbaijan, Russia, Germany, Italy, to name a few. We have selected young players to represent the Republic of Ireland from many areas of this country.

For us, sport is beautiful. Sport is more than sport. Football is more than football. It can be a thing of joy, of intrigue, of amazement. Sport, and in particular football, where the "Team" element becomes more important, can be an educator for life. Teamwork must never be undervalued in life.

Through football, our players learn the values of 'give and take' and winning and losing. In our involvement with young footballers we always emphasise the development of the whole person as well as the football and the tactical skills element.

Developing self esteem, self confidence and self expression are all part of our programme.

Football brings young people together. It opens up the world to them. It also brings up negative issues in themselves and society - prejudice, racism and greed. We try to cultivate respect and not to prejudge - not to be prejudiced. We encourage the skill of understanding. Most of our young footballers have fine Irish role models - Paul McGrath, Niall Quinn, Denis Irwin, Curtis Fleming, to name but a few. Long may it continue!

Is not playing and competing more important than winning?
There will always be winners and losers,
But the real winners are those that 'Have a Go'.

Brian Kerr / Noel O'Reilly,
Irish Underage Soccer Management

The Rich Man and Lazarus

He said to him (the rich man) 'If they do not listen to Moses and the prophets,
neither will they be convinced even if someone rises from the dead.'

Luke, Ch 16, v 31

The only reason it appears the man in this story was excluded from the eternal reward was that he was rich and did not share his wealth with the beggar, Lazarus. By the time he came to die, therefore, he had already received his reward by settling selfishly for the full enjoyment of his riches without reference to the poverty and misery outside his gate. Two thousand years after Jesus has risen from the dead and the "good news for the poor" of the risen Christ has been preached throughout the world, many remain unconvinced that the proper and right way to live, the way to real happiness that will last eternally, is to share the good things one has with the poor. Many, like Lazarus, continue to pay a huge price for the selfishness of the rich in lives of suffering, misery and unfulfilment.

The Lazarus of the parable became the risen Christ who identifies himself totally with the poor (Matthew, Ch. 25, v.31-46) "... for I was hungry and you gave me (or did not give me?) food ..." Do we his followers recognise him? "...when was it that we saw you hungry ..." Can we fail, 2000 years after Christ came among us in the flesh, not to recognise him in the poor and to realise that what we have in terms of material wealth, abilities and talents, are meant to be shared with the poor? If we do recognise our responsibilities, how adequately do we respond or do we simply ignore him? Who are the 'Lazaruses' at our gate that are above all dependent on our generosity to alleviate some of their suffering and to share in some of the comfort we are fortunate enough to enjoy? How happy would we feel in a next life meeting up with them in the presence of Christ and being reminded of our response to their needs?

Lord, give me the grace to recognise those in need that I meet in the course of my life and the ways in which I can help to meet their needs. Then give me the generosity, courage and perseverance daily to make the responses required, difficult and all as it may be, for nothing is impossible with you.

Gerry Mangan,
Member of the Society of St Vincent de Paul

Fiat Justitiae Ruat Coelum.

Let Justice Be Done, Though the Heavens Fall.

This legal maxim can be seen written above the entrance to the Bridewell Garda Station in Chancery Street in Dublin. It implies that the scales of justice, though finely balanced, must not be altered without good and sufficient reason and then only with respect to due process, (i.e. in criminal trials, proof beyond reasonable doubt and in civil proceedings, proof based on the balance of probabilities).

The issue which the policeman or woman of today has to grapple with is to ensure that, in applying and enforcing the provisions of the criminal law, due regard for the common good must be viewed and weighted against the rights of the individual. In extreme cases it may be necessary to consciously decide to exceed statutory provisions and thereby run the risk of breaching individual constitutional rights.

This arose in the case of the State - v - Shaw and Evans, where a suspect was detained beyond the statutory time allowed for the purpose of locating a missing person whose life was clearly in danger. The Supreme Court held that such a decision was both right and proper, as it placed the overall good of the individual's life above that of the suspected person. While such circumstances are likely to be few, they do call for a high degree of informed judgement.

Policing into the new millennium will demand an in-depth knowledge and understanding of poverty, discrimination, exclusion, inequality and other forms of social injustice in order to make informed judgements. Human growth for the policeman or woman is governed in a special way by choice in contrast to the inevitability of the acorn becoming an oak. We grow to maturity through free decisions and choices which make us what we are and will be. John Henry Cardinal Newman spoke rigorously of 'conscience' and 'discernment' in decision making. For those involved in policing, medicine, and a wide range of social work, the challenge of discerning what to do and what not to do in given situations will arise. We should remember that not all such decisions will be guided by statute law and, therefore, we must utilise the combination of learning experience and informed conscience to ensure that justice is achieved in all our dealings with the public.

Members of An Garda Síochána can assist to ease the many social problems which confront us today, but we also need the leadership of the exceptional in all walks of life if we are to overcome social injustice and inequity. People such as Mother Teresa of Calcutta and our own Bob Geldof gave us some insight of how radical solutions can benefit the starving, stricken by famine. I would like to conclude by saying that some social problems are rooted in evil and beyond the capacity of human remedy. In such cases, we must necessarily look to the spiritual influence of prayer to bring about a change of heart.

Pat Byrne,
Garda Commissioner

Community Development and Inequality

The significant thing about the division between rich and poor people, rich and poor nations, is not simply that one has the resources to provide comfort for all its citizens and the other cannot provide basic needs and services. The reality and depth of the problem arises because the one who is rich has power over the lives of those who are poor, and the rich nation has power over the policies of those which are not rich. And even more important is that our social and economic system, nationally and internationally, supports those divisions and constantly increases them, so that the rich get even richer and more powerful, while the poor get relatively poorer and less able to control their own future.

Julius Nyerere, *Freedom and Development*

Imagine organising the economy of a household in such a way that *two* people have unlimited access to personal, social, educational, cultural, economic, political and spiritual development and *eight* people do not. What would we say of such a household?

And yet our world is organised in this way locally, nationally and globally. Twenty per cent of the population own eighty per cent of the wealth. Within this picture there are further inequalities between men and women, different races, people with disabilities, Travellers, Refugees, to name but a few. Now more than ever, we are informed about inequality in its many forms. Knowing inequality exists, however, is not enough to give us a direction to change the situation.

Through the community development process, we are encouraged to participate fully in understanding our reality, in understanding the root causes of poverty and the part we play in perpetuating such an unequal world. We work at creating a vision for an alternative way of living personally, locally, nationally and globally. For such a vision to include equality and justice, it must be one where the energies, resources and potentials of each child, woman and man, each community and each nation, are shared in a co-operative rather than competitive way. Together we must find a way of making this vision a reality day-by-day. Our actions must be based on the respect for the dignity and diversity of all people and their right to participate fully in the solutions to their own realities.

The path of change is difficult. On the one hand we must guard against hopelessness and despair, while on the other, we must avoid aimless activity that deals only with the symptoms of inequality. We have to believe that our contribution to a more responsible and just world is part of a greater movement for change. In the words of John O'Donohue in *Eternal Echoes,* "each one of us is a different light in the emerging collective brightness. A constellation of light has a greater power of illumination than any single light would have on its own. Together, we increase brightness."

ACID

In Jakarta among the vendors, of flowers and soft drinks,
I saw a child with a hideous mouth, begging,
and I knew the wound was made for a way to stay alive.
What I gave him wouldn't keep a dog alive.
What he gave me from the brown coin of his sweating face
was a look of cunning.
I carry it like a bead of acid to remember how,
once in a while, you can creep out of your own life
and become someone else - an explosion in that nest of wires
we call the imagination.
I will never see him again, I suppose,
but what of this rag, this shadow flung like a boy's body
into the walls of my mind, bleeding their sour taste -
insult and anger, the great movers?

Mary Oliver,
New and Selected Poems

Cecilia Forrestal,
Director,
Community Action Network (CAN)

ZERO TOLERANCE ON POVERTY

On the 11 October (1998) *The Sunday Business Post* published a major report, *"Forgotten Angels,"* on St Audeon's school in Cook Street in Dublin's inner city, by its political editor Emily O'Reilly, the finest piece of journalism I have read recently. Here in this report of one hundred and thirty two disadvantaged students and their heroic teachers is revealed in microcosm the dark underlay of poverty that disfigures Ireland's public face. This is a place "where success is measured not in certificates and degrees and cars and professional status but in staying drug free and keeping your children safe".

Here is a place where the poverty trap is set in stone as it is in so many other poverty blackspots around Ireland, north and south. Two points occur to me. Firstly several agencies, for example the Justice Desk of the Conference of Religious of Ireland, the Economic and Social Research Institute and the Simon Community, have revealed the depth of poverty still existing in Ireland. They have made the intellectual case against poverty. Peter McVerry's question in a letter to *The Irish Times* last year still hangs heavily in the air. "If we had £1.8 billion to give away in tax breaks," he asked, "why did a thirteen year old boy with cerebral palsy have to spend a weekend sleeping on the streets because there was no accommodation available?" Governments may run from questions such as these but they cannot hide.

Sometimes, however, the moral clarity of the argument against poverty in our society can get lost in the dizzying welter of statistics. We need works of investigative journalism done responsibly and without prurience, to enflesh the disillusionment, pain and dreary frustration of the marginalised. Am I alone in thinking that our media leaders could do more to encourage questioning journalism? Our newspapers and magazines are growing ever bigger in size, aping America in this as in so much else. They are stuffed with lifestyle supplements on how to spend the fruits of economic victory or columns where certain writers dress up outworn opinions in increasingly outrageous clothes to attract attention. We could do with less intense analyses of our gourmet eateries and more on those seeking to survive on scraps from the Celtic Tiger's table.

Secondly, I believe there is a need for the churches, visionary politicians and the new leaders emerging in Ireland through the area partnerships to work together to strengthen the ethical fabric of our society and to infuse it with a passion for social justice. A useful start might be a campaign to have the proposal of the Irish Commission for Justice and Peace, to have four new rights inserted in the Constitution, adapted - the right to health, the right to adequate housing, the right to adequate nutrition and the right to an adequate standard of living.

It is time we realised that if we develop zero tolerance on poverty
there will be little need for zero tolerance on crime.

Fr Kevin Hegarty,
Shanahee, Belmullet,
Co Mayo

World Debt - Why Jubilee 2000?

And we the housewives ask ourselves: What have we done to incur this foreign debt? Is it possible that our children have eaten too much? Is it possible that they have studied in the best colleges? Have our wages become too great? Together we say: No, no we have not eaten too much. No, we have not dressed any better. We do not have better medical assistance. Then, to whom have the benefits gone? Why are we the ones who have to pay for this debt?

Dominga de Valasquez, Bolivia

Debt is one of the greatest causes of poverty, exclusion, chronic malnutrition and disease, and even death, for about one billion people in what is today called the "Majority World" - those regions where the majority of the world's poorest people live. And none of these people are responsible for it. In the 1970s, when Western banks had enormous amounts of extra cash, due to a sudden rise in oil revenues lodged with them, they persuaded poor country governments to borrow dollars at very low interest rates. Some years later, the United States raised its interest rates from the very low base of three per cent to twenty-one per cent, and the debt crisis began immediately. Since then, these countries, obeying instructions from the International Monetary Fund and the World Bank acting on behalf of the rich "North", have been sacrificing all growth to the priority of paying back their loans.

Not all the borrowed dollars had been spent foolishly. All progressive social, educational and health programmes were cut to minimise public expenditure, with results to which Dominga de Valasquez testifies graphically. It is estimated that over 500,000 children die each year because of cut backs to health services. And the precious forests, rivers and wild life are being destroyed at an alarming speed. This scandalous situation has provoked Pope John Paul II and many other leaders of churches to call for the debt to be cancelled, so that the poor can have a fresh start.

God has always taken the side of the poor. The Bible is very clear about this. We have been created in the image of God, which means that we humans should reflect God's love, passionate concern and caring for one another. This means that injustice must be redressed. In the Old Testament this happened at the Jubilee Year, every fifty years.

Christians today are calling for a new Jubilee in the year 2000, so that debts would be forgiven, those enslaved by poverty and degradation be freed, and the earth restored to its beauty. Jesus, whose Great Commandment was "Love one another as I have loved you", came that all might have life "to the full". We follow Jesus and remain his disciples if we share his concerns for the poorest in our midst, both at home and abroad, that they may have their rightful share in the earth's resources. One concrete and effective step would be to make sure to sign the *Jubilee 2000 Petition for Debt Cancellation*, addressed to the leaders of the world's richest nations, before June 1999.

Jesus, give us your eyes to look out on our world, your ears to hear the cries of the poorest,
your heart to experience your anger at injustice and your compassion for all who suffer
and give us your will to change what needs to be changed, both within us and around us,
so that we might all become one family on an earth that reflects your wisdom and beauty.

Sr Carol Dorgan,
Little Sisters of the Assumption, Ballymun

Farawayan

However much I love you, however much I feel for you,
however much I want to make you feel at home,
I can't Faraya so I can't....
I have to send you home again to Farawaya,
home Faraya, farawaya home,
home Faraya, farawaya home ...

Queen Maud to asylum-seeker Faraya in *Farawayan*

Refugees and vulnerable immigrants have been targeted in Ireland in the past two years in much the same way as the Jews were in Nazi Germany in the early 1930s. It is a gradual seeping attitude, an isolation strategy, that generates an atmosphere where it's okay to say the most brutish things about people. And the step from saying to doing is an inevitable step. Are we going to make them wear striped uniforms, or at least an identifiable crest? It makes sense, after all - the accounts books say so. And in Ireland today, with regard to refugees, unless we alter course radically, the accounts book is our guiding moral. Meanwhile, our sense of shared humanity is in smithereens - a shattered mirror underneath our jackbooted feet.

Farawayan is the title of a theatre piece I wrote and directed, produced by Calypso Productions in the Olympic Theatre, Dublin, in autumn 1998. It was about the experience of being treated as a Farawayan - a person from faraway. In Farawayan, the refugee Faraya is deported in a straight jacket. We thought we were using the device of dramatic exaggeration. We were not. We were copying reality.

On the night we opened in Dublin, a Nigerian girl called Semira Adamu was suffocated to death in Brussels airport by immigration officials who gagged her to stifle her screams as they deported her. How long before a deportee suffers a similar fate in Ireland as Semira Adamu did that night in Brussels, the capital of the European Union?

Is there ever a circumstance where binding and gagging someone is justified?
Is a regulation which provides for such measures excusable?

Donal O'Kelly,
Playwright

What kind of Ireland do we want?

It remains to be seen which will win: the spirit of selfishness or the spirit of sacrifice. Will society merely develop into a means of exploitation for the strongest members to make huge profits or will everyone devote themselves to the common good and especially the protection of the weak? It is our duty to throw ourselves between these opposing armies. We might not be able to prevent their confrontation but at least we can help to absorb some of the shock.

Blessed Frederick Ozanam: 13 November 1836, aged 23

These words of the principal founder of the Society of St Vincent de Paul have an extraordinary relevance to contemporary Ireland. We live in a society that is powering ahead economically but many do not benefit from that growth and remain excluded. The gap between the rich and the poor is widening. Is this the kind of Ireland we want? If not, what can be done? The challenge for us in the Society of St Vincent de Paul is to make more widely known what our members are encountering when they visit the homes of those who are poor - and see the despair of men and women who, through lack of education, literacy or skills, can never benefit from job opportunities; the children whose home environment is such that they have little chance of remaining in education; the communities devastated by substance abuse - itself an outcome of years of neglect and high unemployment. Many would not believe that such conditions could exist in the prosperous Ireland of today. We have to make what we see known to the public at large, for in a democracy like ours, public opinion is a powerful influence on politicians. We have to make it known to government as an issue of social justice and help shape the targeted intervention that is now so desperately needed to help many out of poverty and exclusion. In the allocation of the buoyant government revenues we must insist that there be a preferential option for those who are poor and excluded.

While government action is central to creating a society where the gap between the haves and have nots is narrowed, we should also ask ourselves what we as individuals can do. Are we willing to pay the price in terms of say, public sector pay restraint; or acceptance of a slower drop in income tax rates in the interest of transfers to the worse off? Are we willing to face the fact that those of us who may be reasonably well off are part of the problem? Do we really want to be part of the solution?

Larry Tuomey, President,
Dublin Regional Council SVP

The Fundamental Poverty

Now I see the secret of the making of the best persons.
It is to grow in the open air, and to eat and sleep with the earth.

Walt Whitman, *Leaves of Grass.*

In 1904 the Congested Districts Board gave a two-bedroom, stone-built cottage, a byre and thirty one acres of land to a family as part of its programme to deal with poverty in rural Ireland. To-day I live in that cottage, aware of its origins and grateful for the vision of its instigators. For me the essence of human wholeness and fulfilment is an engagement with the elemental in nature - light and darkness, death and birth, cycles and seasons, sowing and harvesting, story and calm, abundance and scarcity. This engagement with the inevitability of nature is at once challenging and invigorating. It exposes things as they are, rather than as they are said to be. It nourishes a sense of place, space and belonging. A broader and more complex image of humankind emerges and a consciousness of the interconnectedness between all creation is awakened. It invites people to become more aware of and take greater responsibility for their own actions. It puts people in touch with their needs and challenges them to a creative response to meeting these needs. In this sense work and creativity become integral aspects of human living. The absence of an elemental dimension to the lives of people is a significant deprivation and one which in the long run takes its toll on individuals, groups and societies. It is the fundamental poverty of our age.

Modern society has developed an organisational system where the natural, organic habitat of human beings is replaced by a one-dimensional and simplified environment where there is little opportunity to engage with the elemental. Work and creativity have become external to the individual, giving rise to a split between being and having. Where affluence and prosperity abide the poverty of such environments and ways of living may be masked for the time being by image, appearance and the seduction of materialism and acquisitiveness. Where material deprivation persists, the uprootedness may be more apparent as people evidently live their lives in various states of anomie and alienation.

Do our present policies with the emphasis on high density housing, large shopping malls and centralisation of services create a climate conducive to people engaging with the elemental in nature?

Does our growing reliance on others for most of our basic requirements - food, shelter, work and health care - contribute to a sense of wholeness in individuals?

What are the implications of the prevailing ethos of individual acquisition and materialism for individuals, communities and societies exploring more holistic ways of relating with nature, with themselves and with the source of being?

Is the image of humankind which sees humans as controlling nature rather than working in harmony with it in the best interests of human well-being and self–realisation?

What are the implications of current approaches to work and employment for human beings whose natural inclination is to work and to be creative in their daily living?

A new paradigm is required. How can this come about?

Last night the moon peeped out
For an instant in full salute to passing
Pilgrims marking time to affirm
That all was still well and unfolding.
The universal order of seasons and
Cycles coming and going unfailingly
To wax and wane in orbit predictable
All the while inviting our response.

Night lamp for illumination and hope
Guardian of dreams present and to come
Ruler of tides for daily equilibrium
Governing movement of life force
To maintain the elemental nature of
Things restoring and renewing to
Bring menstrual healing to planet.
Earth/air/fire/water and me.

Michael Browne,
Writer

Do the Poor Count?

Amen, I say to you, as long as you did it to one of these my least brethren, you did it to me.

Matthew, Ch 25, v40

In the mid 1990s, due to a shortage of housing sites in Dublin City, the Corporation was forced to buy individual houses in settled private estates. This policy was vigorously opposed and effectively defeated by many Residents' Associations, who were in turn supported by local politicians from the main political parties.

Indeed, certain 'pro-life' politicians were prominent in opposing the Corporation's attempts to house needy families in private houses. Some of the families housed in this way were treated very badly by some of their new neighbours. Children were taunted for being 'from the Corporation' and not owning their home.

How many of those people, leading lights in their Residents' Associations, went to Mass on Sundays? What did the Mass and their declared belief in Jesus Christ mean to them? Why did no local clergy defend the Corporation's policy? Were they fearful of alienating their flock? What happened to our Christian Charity that no one could say: let us welcome the few less fortunate families and their children into our community? I remain unable to understand what I witnessed at that time.

How can politicians and other people reconcile a 'pro life' stance with active successful efforts to exclude the less fortunate children/families in our society from the chance of a home of their own?

"Amen I say to you, as long as you did it not to one of these least, neither did you do it to me."
Matthew, Ch 25, v 25

Tony Gregory, T.D.,
Dublin North Central

Partnership for Progress?

You don't become poor in Ireland, you remain poor.

When people ask about poverty in Ireland they look for someone to blame. Everyone is keen to point the finger, particularly at the people themselves. In reality it is a structural problem which sees large groups of people born into poverty. They and their children remain there - fifteen per cent of the population of Ireland, believe it or not.

The era of Social Partnership is offering an opportunity to change this. We have Local Area Based Partnerships, National Economic and Social Council, National Economic and Social Forum, National Anti Poverty Strategy and, crucially, Partnership 2000. National Agreements are all about consensus - the beginnings of working together.

These agreements between government, employers, farmers, unions and most recently, the community and voluntary sector, are consensus agreements, a way of working together for the common good. Priorities are set, costed, evaluated, compared with each other, and eventually graded in order of importance by those who ultimately call the shots, the government and, more often than not, their wealthy backers.

What is gratifying is the process, how all this is done and the effect that working together brings. The process means that a great deal of listening takes place, space is created for each group to lay out its stall, to have its goods examined, challenged and evaluated by friend and foe. The process is the building of an understanding of each group's position. This understanding leads to inclusion of their ideas and the recognition that their views are worthwhile, but when push comes to shove, the process must have a result, a consensus which often waters down the strength of the arguments and the principles behind them, but opens doors to developing working relationships which will benefit the excluded in the long term.

What has all of this achieved now for those who live in poverty? Very little in concrete terms. The problems all remain as they were ten years ago. The system has been tweaked and rationalised, innovative schemes have been introduced, the strength of the economy has raised some boats, but poverty is still there. Why? It is embedded in the structures. For this to change, the power base within the Partnership must change. Yes, people recognise the validity of our arguments. They see the statistics, but they are not ready to make it safe for government to redistribute wealth to ensure the elimination of poverty. That's where you, the reader, come in. It is not about political arguments, policies, or programmes for government. It is not about what benefits you personally. It is about the right of fifteen per cent of our people living below the poverty line to be part of our society. That's not a debate. No one has a right to a view about this. We are either Christian or we are not.

Liam O'Dwyer,
Administrator, Dublin Region, SVP

Suggestions for Group Reflection

The following points may be useful if you wish to use these reflections for groups or for community reflection.

1. Call the group into reflection with a period of slience.

2. Get one or more members to read the first part of the Reflection.
   Stop where it makes sense.
   In some cases it makes sense to read the full text.

3. It might be a good idea if somebody prepared the reading/reflection beforehand.

4. Allow time for some discussion or reflection.
   Rushing is the enemy of reflection.

5. The group might end with a resolution or an appropriate individual/group action.

6. The tried and tested model "See, Judge, Act" may be useful for groups.

MISSION STATEMENT
for a New Millennium

Mission Statement

The Society of St Vincent de Paul is a Christian lay voluntary organisation, working with the poor and disadvantaged. Inspired by our principal founder, Frederic Ozanam and our patron, St Vincent de Paul, we seek to respond to the call every Christian receives to bring the love of Christ to those we serve in the spirit of the gospel message: 'I was hungry and you gave me to eat ...' (Matthew, Ch.25).

No work of charity is foreign to the Society. We are involved in a diverse range of activities characterised by:

Support & friendship: Through person to person contact, we are committed to respecting the dignity of those we assist and thus to fostering their self-respect. In the provision of material and other support, we assure confidentiality at all times and endeavour to establish relationships based on trust and friendship.

Promoting self-sufficiency: We believe it is not enough to provide short-term material support. Those we serve must also be helped to achieve self-sufficiency in the longer term and the sense of self-worth this provides. When the problems we encounter are beyond our competence, we build bridges of support with others more specialised.

Working for social justice: We are committed to identifying the root causes of poverty and social injustice in Ireland and, in solidarity with the poor and disadvantaged, to advocate and work for the changes required to create a more just and caring society.

Designed @ Language